"All my love to you, Amy…Carry on."
James Taylor
Grammy Award–winning musician

"Thank you, Mike Nappa, for the privilege of being able to share in Amy's journey home. Your openness and vulnerability will be a blessing to all who read *Hard Way Home*! Amy's last chapter continues…"
Karen Pence
Second Lady of the United States

"Half of all married couples will someday experience the death of their spouse. *Hard Way Home* is a powerful, raw account of one couple's journey. It demonstrates the value of extended family, friends, tears, laughter, and a strong faith in God. Without these, the journey will be much more difficult. If you are taking the hard way home, you will find encouragement here. If you are a friend of one who is walking that road, it will remind you that there is no greater gift than friendship."
Gary Chapman, PhD
#1 *New York Times* bestselling author of *The Five Love Languages*

"Amy Nappa touched my life in so many positive ways. I am very sorry for her loss, but I know Amy lives on in all our hearts. I frequently have 'talks' with my departed patients as I find it a source of comfort and peace. Amy has joined my 'pack of angels' upstairs. Peace and love to all who were blessed to know her."
Jennifer Rubatt, MD
director of gynecologic oncology, Banner Health

"Whew! What an incredibly touching read. *Hard Way Home* is a candid love story of a beautiful battle. It will move you. Inspire you. And in the words of one of Amy's friends, it will 'brighten up even your darkest nights.'"
Les and Leslie Parrott
#1 *New York Times* bestselling authors of *Saving Your Marriage Before It Starts*

"Hope you had great adventures together…and will have many more."
Pete Docter
Academy Award–winning filmmaker

Hard Way Home

AMY *and* MIKE NAPPA

HARVEST HOUSE PUBLISHERS
EUGENE, OREGON

Cover design by John Hamilton Design

Cover photo © Luca Pierro / Stocksy

Unless otherwise indicated, all interior photos are © Nappaland Communications Inc. Used by permission.

Hospital photo of Amy Nappa on page 231 with the caption "Sunday, September 11, 2016" by Jody Brolsma. Used by permission.

Published in association with Nappaland Literary Agency, a division of Nappaland Communications Inc. Visit us at www.Nappaland.com.

Events in this book are true and factual, though a few names have been changed. Any errors or misstatements in this book are accidental and subject to correction in a future printing.

Hard Way Home
Copyright © 2019 Nappaland Communications Inc.
Published by Harvest House Publishers
Eugene, Oregon 97408
www.harvesthousepublishers.com
ISBN 978-0-7369-7677-0 (hardcover)
ISBN 978-0-7369-7678-7 (eBook)
Library of Congress Cataloging-in-Publication Data
Names: Nappa, Mike, 1963- author. | Nappa, Amy, 1963- author.
Title: Hard way home / Mike Nappa and Amy Nappa.
Description: Eugene, Oregon : Harvest House Publishers, [2019]
Identifiers: LCCN 2018025418 (print) | LCCN 2018026015 (ebook) | ISBN
   9780736976787 (ebook) | ISBN 9780736976770 (hardcover)
Subjects: LCSH: Nappa, Amy, 1963—Health. | Nappa, Mike, 1963- |
   Uterus—Cancer—Patients—United States—Biography. |
   Uterus—Cancer—Patients—Family relationships. | Husband and
   wife—Religious aspects—Biography.
Classification: LCC RC280.U8 (ebook) | LCC RC280.U8 N35 2019 (print) | DDC
   616.99/466—dc23
LC record available at https://lccn.loc.gov/2018025418

Printed in the United States of America

19 20 21 22 23 24 25 26 27 / Bang-SK / 10 9 8 7 6 5 4 3 2 1

Your touch on the lives of others is like the touch of no one else. The "fingerprints" you leave on someone's heart can be traced back to no one but you.

AMY NAPPA,
A WOMAN'S TOUCH

The Facts About Cancer in America

At any given time, roughly 15 million
of us are living with cancer.

This year alone, more than 1.6 million
of us will be diagnosed with cancer.

More than a third of us will be
diagnosed with cancer in our lifetimes.

And…

cancer will kill more than 600,000
of us before this year ends.[1]

---

1. From the National Institutes of Health, "Cancer Stat Facts: Cancer of Any Site," National Cancer Institute, https://seer.cancer.gov/statfacts/html/all.html.

Contents

Foreword

James Taylor

[Author's note: On May 25, 2016, international music legend James Taylor took time out from a North America concert tour to send a personal video message to Amy Nappa. All he knew of her was that she was dying of cancer and that she had hundreds of friends who had begged him to make her smile.

So he did. And she did indeed smile.

Mr. Taylor's outrageous kindness had Amy smiling—and bragging—for weeks about "My new best friend, JAMES TAYLOR!" He and his assistant Ellyn were, and continue to be, the kindest, most thoughtful, and generous of people. They get many requests like ours and simply can't respond to them all. We are grateful they made an exception for Amy.

And now James Taylor has done us one more unmerited favor, allowing us to share with you the contents of his message to Amy as the foreword to this book.

Again, we are grateful.]

"For Amy, from James"

Hi, Amy,

It's James Taylor here, in my studio at home in Western Massachusetts. We have a few days off from the tour, just sort of recuperating in my home space here a little bit.

Mike got in touch with Ellyn, my friend and assistant, and told me about your situation and that you were a fan who had listened for many years and were hoping maybe to get out and see this particular tour. I guess the closest we're coming to you is probably Tucson, but Mike says that that window has closed, that you can't make it. So I just thought I'd send you a video salute, just tell you that we've been thinking about you. A lot.

Words fail me.

Obviously it's hard to drop in casually to something as deep, and profound, and extreme as what you're experiencing. But I wanted to let you know that I'm thinking about you and wishing you all the best. I send you love, and light, and just enjoyment of what life has given to us.

All my love to you, Amy. Love from Ellyn, from everybody here, and...

Carry on.

"For James, from Amy!"

Hello, James,

I'm the one you recently sent a video to—after being bombarded with messages from my husband and many friends. I can't even begin to tell you how much that video meant to me. It's my own dang fault for thinking I would always have a chance to see you in concert—and here I am trying to get through my bucket list, and you are the final thing on it!

Thank you for your kindness and for taking the time to encourage me on this journey. Cancer is a cruel dragon, but I have never felt alone in my fight. My friends and faith in God have carried me along and hold me up when I feel I can't fight. While I still have hope that I might recover enough to have a few more years, I also face the brutal realities of my situation.

Kindnesses like yours toward me bring me joy and delight.

Thank you again!
Amy!
June 7, 2016

If you'd like to see a video of the first time Amy watched her message from James Taylor, you'll find it online at AmyNappa.com.

> **James Taylor** is an international music legend and author of time-less hit songs, like "Fire and Rain," "Carolina in My Mind," "You've Got a Friend," and "Song for You Far Away." Mr. Taylor has sold more than 100 million albums and won five Grammy Awards. And he's just a good guy—so, you know, he's got that going for him.

Prelude

S he dies at the end.

I think you should know that up front—so you are prepared, so you know what you're getting into.

I was tempted not to tell you, to keep it a mystery. After all, when we lived this moment, we didn't know at first whether she would survive or die. Why should it be any different for you? But I've learned from experience that it's hard to watch death creeping toward someone you love, not knowing whether it's just peeking or planning to walk in and stay awhile. And I think you are going to love my wife, so I wanted to give you fair warning:

Our girl dies in the end.

I should also tell you why we call Amy "our girl," because you'll see that quite a bit in this book.

Early in our marriage, I used to call Amy "my best girl," and somewhere along the decades it got shortened to just "my girl." It was kind of my nickname for her whenever I needed an excuse to do something fun or buy something I knew she'd want. "My girl says I need to look pretty for the Christmas party," I'd say flippantly, or "My girl wants chocolate ice cream, so she gets chocolate ice cream." It made me happy to talk about Amy this way, and I think she liked it too. And then, as the months passed from 2015 into 2016, I realized the truth about my girl…

Turns out she belonged to more people than I could have imagined! She'd filled the hearts and lives of so many people that one day during chemotherapy, I finally understood she was not just "my girl." To hundreds and hundreds of caring friends and coworkers—and even to people she barely knew—she was "our girl." And she still is.

So this book is about what happened to our girl—as it happened—after Amy was unexpectedly diagnosed with stage IV-B uterine cancer. I didn't know I was writing this book when I wrote it. I thought I was just keeping a few friends and family members up to date on Amy's medical situation (and her occasional Disney obsession).

See, a few days before her first surgery, Amy was stressed about keeping our family and a few close friends updated on her condition, so I said, "I'll take care of it." That was my husband code for "Don't worry your pretty little head about it; you just concentrate on fighting this deadly cancer."

To make sure she wouldn't worry, that night I started a secret Facebook group called "Amy! Makes Me Smile." (Yes, our girl always spelled her name with an exclamation point, and yes, it fit her well.) I put about 20 people in the group and informed Amy I'd just tell everyone the truth about whatever happened, and we'd all find our way through it somehow.

What I didn't realize was that there were a lot more than 20 people who loved Amy and wanted to walk beside her through this whole cancer journey.

More of her friends asked to be added to the group, then more, and then so many I lost count of them all. And then they started copying my updates and sending them out to all their friends too. (No, I guess they didn't understand what the word "secret" meant in "Facebook secret group.") In the end there were hundreds of "friends" in this supposedly secret group, and thousands more were reading daily about Amy's fight with cancer on Facebook—most of whom I still don't know. But they knew Amy, and they loved her with a determination I've never seen before or since. They loved her all the way to the finish line and became an immense source of strength for her as she suffered.

Yeah, those people are pretty cool.

And so that's what the bulk of this book is—updates from "Amy! Makes Me Smile" on Facebook along with a few letters from Amy's journal, which I've added at the end.

I struggled with the decision of whether to publish this book, and I'll tell you why. When you turn the pages in here, my girl will just be a character in a story to you, almost a beautiful little fiction to pass your Sunday afternoon. To me she was indescribably more.

Amy! was a living, breathing, breathtaking soul who for 30 years inhabited and influenced every moment of my existence. She was my laughter and my heartbreak, my joy and my confidante, my playmate and my errand buddy, my breath and my courage to start each new day. Amy's hands held me up, wiped away my tears, and strengthened my weakening bones. Amy's emerald eyes made me understand what beauty looked like. Her smile gave me purpose in life. Her existence reminded me every day that God is very much alive—and very much involved in the smallest details of me.

Amy was to me—to my heart, body, and soul—the closest thing to heaven I'll ever see with my own eyes or touch with my own lips.[1]

Try to remember that for me, will you?

Remember that my girl was not just a beautiful story for you to read about, but an irreplaceable gift from God into my often bleary and sin-sick world.

---

1. Yes, of course, I know I will see and touch her again when I leave this earth and join her in heaven—but you know what I mean. We're not here to parse theology today; we can do that in another book, at another time, OK?

Knowing you are doing that, I think, will help me just a little as I tell you what happened to her. To us.

All right. Enough with the long-winded prelude. Just one last thing and then we'll get started.

Before she went into hospice, I made Amy write her own obituary. I just couldn't bring myself to do it. Here's what she wrote, how she wanted to be remembered:

> **Amy Wakefield Nappa** was born on November 10, 1963, in Portsmouth, Virginia, to Norm and Winnie Wakefield. She moved to heaven on September 11, 2016. Amy was a sister, a wife, a mother, grandmother, and friend. She loved her family and her friends dearly. Her greatest joys were to spend time with family, to hang out with her friends, to laugh, and to mentor those a little behind her in the journey of life. Amy loved Jesus with all her heart, and her greatest desire was to be remembered as a woman who shined the love of Jesus.

1

'Twas the Night Before Disneyland...

Keep me safe, my God,
for in you I take refuge.
I say to the LORD,
"You are my Lord; apart from you
I have no good thing."

PSALM 16:1-2

AMY! MAKES ME SMILE

Mike Nappa created this group on August 15, 2015

Secret Group

Description: This group is for friends of Amy who want to keep up to date on her medical situation (and occasional Disney obsession).

Admins: Mike Nappa, Amy Nappa

Saturday, August 15, 2015

Hi, all—welcome to the Amy! Makes Me Smile group. Here's the latest update:

At this point, most of you know that Amy has been diagnosed with cancer. We're still not sure if it's ovarian cancer or abdominal cancer, but the doctors have run a billion tests, and we're supposed to get more info next week. We had planned a big trip to Disneyland this month—in fact, we're supposed to be there right now. We were going to leave on August 13, attend the D23 Expo in Anaheim, meet a few Disney celebrities, and spend a day being goofballs in Disneyland Park. Imagine our shock when, on August 12, with bags packed, Amy was diagnosed with cancer. Anyway...

Key dates ahead:

Tuesday: We meet Amy's oncologist and have the "real" cancer discussion. We are nervous about this but also relieved to finally be moving forward in tackling the problem.

Wednesday: Surgery! Not an exciting event, but again, we're glad to be attacking the problem instead of wondering what we should do.

That's all we know right now. We are continuing to see God's grace every day in this situation, and Amy is maintaining good spirits—though she is apprehensive about the upcoming surgery and recovery period. We welcome your prayers.

Love you all!

P.S. For the record, Amy didn't cry when they told her she had cancer. She cried when I told her she couldn't go to Disneyland.

Monday, August 17, 2015

Hi, all,

OK, surgery is scheduled for Wednesday August 19, at 7:30 a.m. Amy says she'll post more info here a little bit later, but right now it looks like she'll be out for about six weeks after surgery.

Later...

I'm looking for two volunteers who are willing to fast and pray for Amy:

- one person who will fast and pray from sunrise to sunset tomorrow (Tuesday, August 18) and

- one who will fast and pray from sunrise to sunset on Wednesday (August 19).

Is anyone available? Let me know—thanks![1]

Tuesday, August 18, 2015

Hi, all!

Today we finally meet the oncologist for the first time! We are nervous but also grateful to be going into this meeting with your prayers and love. We have a list of questions, and I'll be sure to update you later this afternoon if we learn anything new.

We love you!

Later...

"I know whom I have believed, and am convinced that he is able to guard what I have entrusted to him until that day" (2 Timothy 1:12).

Later...

(From Amy!)

We just got back from the oncologist's office. She spent more than an hour with us explaining everything. I won't go into every detail, but the fluid they drew from me last week does show cancer cells, and the marker for ovarian cancer that they found in my blood is super, super elevated (like, it's

---

1. More than two dozen people volunteered to fast and pray. My friend who is an atheist (or agnostic—I get them confused) said that even though he didn't believe in prayer, he still wanted to support Amy. So he fasted along with the rest of Amy's friends. Which I thought was pretty cool.

supposed to be 35, and it's over 3,400). They are going to go in and take out my ovaries and all the cancer. She may have to take out other stuff, like my appendix—just depends on what she finds when she gets in there. She said I will start chemo in about four weeks. She may insert a port during the surgery that would allow them to give me chemo directly to the affected areas—that would be her first choice, but she will determine if I am a good candidate for that when she is doing the surgery.

The cancer is at stage III-C.[2] This is not good...but it is also not the worst. The good part is that I am young and in good health, so they think that will help me a lot.

Please keep praying for me. I'm not thrilled with this news, but I am also not devastated. I have peace.

I won't be able to have visitors tomorrow except my family. Mike will post on Thursday if I can see anyone by then. Check back for updates—he will keep posting.

Later...

Amy is resting quietly now. Before she went to sleep, she said to me, "I am resting in God's hands." We not only believe that; we know it to be true.

Tomorrow begins the adventure. We are grateful to have you nearby for the long journey ahead.

We love you!

---

2. This stage III-C assessment wasn't correct, but we didn't know that at the time. Turned out that Amy's cancer was more advanced than any of us had imagined, even the doctors. This early diagnosis was later revised to be cancer at stage IV-B, which was pretty close to the worst it could be.

Hard Way Home

Wednesday, August 19, 2015

(From Amy!)

Good morning, everyone! It was one week ago today that I learned I have cancer, and reading through Facebook last night and this morning—and the number of texts and calls I have received—I simply can't tell you all how loved I feel facing today and the coming days. I just feel like love is pouring over me! I am honored to have every one of you as my friend.

I leave in a few minutes for the hospital and will not see your posts for a few days. Mike will keep you updated.

Please pray for Dr. Jennifer Rubatt and her associate as they operate today. Please pray for the staff at McKee as they care for me and for so many others today. Please pray for my family—both those who are here with me and those who are far away and wish they were near. Please pray they get the IV in on the first try—I am not a fan of needles!

For a while last night, when I couldn't sleep, I sang VBS songs.[3] They continue to go through my mind this morning—and I can go back a lot of years! "I will not be afraid, though trouble's out there, both night and day...You're powerful! I will hold on to my faith...My God is powerful...I will hold on to him." (Anyone recognize any of those?)

So today, sing a VBS song loud and clear. Shanny, Cindy, and Patty can lead you in the motions. Sing your trust in God and have joy in your heart as you join with me in this! Our God is powerful!

---

3. The company where Amy worked, Group Publishing, produced a Vacation Bible School (VBS) curriculum every year. Although Amy didn't work directly on VBS stuff (her sister Jody Brolsma is in charge of that department), she loved working with kids, so she always volunteered for every VBS field test. She was the official "Imagination Station" leader every year, and she always added a bit of Disney-style flair to it. She loved volunteering for VBS, and they all loved having her there too.

Later...

Amy is in surgery right now. All seems to be going well. While you are praying, I thought you might enjoy a little levity from Amy's cheer squad last night...[4]

Later...

Amy is out of surgery. They were not able to get all the tumors out but did get the largest ones. Too many tiny ones to remove without damage, so they'll treat those with chemo. For now she is doing well. We are just waiting for her to wake up. Thank you for your prayers!

Later...

OK, here's the latest. Amy is in the intensive care unit at the hospital, so no visitors except immediate family unless otherwise approved, and even

---

4. This is Amy with her buddy Genevieve, our granddaughter, who was two and a half years old at the time. Amy wasn't feeling great, so Genevieve climbed up on the couch to play with her.

immediate family should not stay longer than ten minutes at a time (she wears out very quickly). Also, no children visitors in intensive care—let's wait until Amy is stronger and in her own room, as her current condition might be scary for children who love her.

They are telling me that Amy will be in the ICU for two days or until "her bowel wakes up," however long that will be. After that, she will be moved to a regular room, where she will stay for about five more days. When she gets to a regular room, I'll let you know about expanded visits.

And just because I think you want to know this, Amy's doctor is apparently the equivalent of surgical mixed martial arts (MMA). The largest tumor stretched from side to side across Amy's bowel. Dr. Rubatt didn't want to damage Amy's bowel, so to get the tumor off, she wedged her fingers between the tumor and the bowel and then, in her words, "peeled it off by hand." Ewwww! And awesome!

We love you guys!

Later…

By the way—for those who are keeping track of these things—the first person Amy asked for when she woke up was not me…not her father…not her mother…but Jody. Guess nothing gets between a girl and her sisters, right?

Thursday, August 20, 2015

Hello, all,

We are so grateful for your love and support. Amy smiles when she talks about you.

She is doing well but is still very weak. She is determined to get out of the ICU, though, so she can have "real" visitors.

For now, though, please don't come by the hospital to see her. She needs to build up her strength, and hosting visitors (even though she loves it) is a physical drain on her. However, I promise to let everyone know when it's OK to come by and shower Amy with love in person.

Meantime, we still covet your prayers and words of encouragement. Every so often Amy wakes up and says to me, "Read me what people are saying on Facebook."

I will update you again shortly with more on Amy's physical condition. We love you!

Later...

Nurse just delivered a package. Amy now has a lifetime supply of ChapStick. Thanks, Cheryl! Oh wait, Amy says that's only enough to last until Tuesday...

Later...

Amy is unexpectedly running a fever. The nurse took her temperature twice because he was surprised by the first reading. Also, her lung capacity is decreasing as the day goes on instead of increasing.

Ready...set...pray!

Later...

OK, here's what we're asking God for Amy today:

1. Strength!

Amy is in good spirits but still very weak. She is awake and alert more often but typically doesn't last more than ten minutes or so before saying, "I need to close my eyes." She tried to sit up on the edge of the bed this morning and pretty much passed out from the effort. The nurse thinks that her medication may have contributed to that, so she lowered the dosage, which we think will help—but which also increases Amy's pain. So we are praying that God's Holy Spirit will fill her physical body with new strength and stamina and health.

2. Gas!

OK, now some of you are sorry you asked to be added to this group, aren't you? But this is a serious request. The surgical anesthesia caused Amy's bowel to go dormant, meaning she is not able to process food or water at this point. (She's on an IV for nutrition.) As the doctor said, "We need her bowel to wake up" and begin moving so she can eat and drink again. The first sign of that is passing gas through the bowel—it's an extremely important early marker of recovery. So as the T-shirt says, "Make Supplication for Ventilation." (OK, no T-shirt really says that, but you get the idea.)

3. Breath!

Amy's lungs are also affected by the anesthesia and are not working at full capacity. They've given her some exercises to do today in hope of strengthening her lungs. She needs the oxygen in her bloodstream to promote healing, and she also needs her lungs to be fully functional so fluid doesn't build up in there. The goal is for her to be able to inhale 2,500 (insert some random nonsensical hospital term here) before the end of the day. She is at 1,200 right now, so we are praying Jesus will fill her lungs with breath and life and health and hope.

4. Thanks!

Dr. Rubatt says Amy is ahead of schedule so far and that Amy is in good shape for postsurgery, with vital signs all in good numbers. There is even the hope that Amy might be able to move out of the ICU by tomorrow. (We'll see! We hope!) On Amy's dresser is a beautiful lavender plant that makes her smile every time she looks at it as well as a large vase filled with two dozen stunning long-stem roses. Just beautiful. Additionally, Amy is happy to have a tube of "mouth moisturizer" (a ChapStick-like thing she can rub on her tongue) to help with dryness in her mouth since she can't drink anything. Best of all, the doctor agreed to take out the plastic tube going down Amy's throat, which made Amy very happy. She hated the discomfort of that tube. However, that tube was protecting her dormant bowel, so now that the tube is gone, we really need Amy's bowel to wake up. (Supplication for Ventilation!)

All right! Now you know everything I know. In case we haven't mentioned it, we love you very much and are so grateful for your kindness, generosity, and love toward us.

Ready…set…pray!

Later…

Hi, all,

Just a quick update. Amy is resting but feeling more pain. She says she is having muscle spasms in her abdomen, and she's trying to sleep. She's exhausted from the day, which I think adds to it. Also, she's trying to wean herself from extra pain medicine bursts, which means she's making herself endure a little more than she has to, but that's the way she wants it. She's a strong-willed girl (understatement of the month!). She's still not able to breathe deeply, but she keeps trying to do her exercises. She maintains good spirits and says to tell you that she loves you all.

Later…

(From Amy!)

Hey, everyone. I'm awake for a few minutes. Trying to sit up and do my breathing exercise. I do have pain but nothing I can't tolerate. I have the option for more pain medicine, so I can take that when I need to.

Getting the tube out of my nose and throat was a huge relief. That thing was gall-dang miserable!

Thank you for love and prayers. I love you all!

Friday, August 21, 2015

OK, first of all, I feel sorry for anyone who doesn't live in northern Colorado today. Blue sky, soft wind, clean air, bright morning. Makes you want to just stop, breathe deeply, and listen to God's presence whispering sweet nothings in your ear.

So you know, if you don't live in Loveland today, then it sucks to be you.

Anyway, Amy had a solid night and a good morning. Still no farts (working on it!), but we're beginning to see signs that the bowel is starting to gurgle back toward consciousness. She has been allowed to have small amounts of liquids this morning, and they are waiting to see if that will work its way through.

Amy was awake for more than an hour this morning, which is kind of a big deal, as it signals she is getting stronger. Yesterday, just talking to someone for five minutes wore her out so much that she'd fall into a deep sleep right after. She is sleeping now, but she earned it!

When I arrived this morning, she was like a kindergarten child with her enthusiasm. "Go out into the hall," she ordered. When I was standing outside the door, she called out, "See that big plant?" Sure enough, down the hall, 30 feet away, was a gangly green potted plant standing sentry. "I walked all the way there and back!" We cheered, of course. That kind of thing is big news for people like us today. Yes, I made the call to the Associated Press.

At Amy's insistence, they are trying to wean her off the epidural pain medicine. She says the epidural is uncomfortable. Plus I think she just hates depending on something outside her like that. She's so competitive. (Another understatement of the month, right?) At any rate, they're trying oral pain medicine instead but keeping the epidural hooked up in case she has any trouble handling the oral medicine. We especially don't want her to get nauseated from it because throwing up would cause her lots of abdominal pain and could tear at her scar. (Update here: She did not throw up! Yay! But the pain medicine wasn't strong enough, so after a bit they had to turn on the epidural again. Ah, well. They said they'll try again later.)

She still doesn't breathe well, not deeply enough, but she's working on it with the determination of a BodyFlow class addict. (Did I mention she's a little competitive? I don't think any of you knew that about her. Ahem.)

So all in all, a good morning so far, but there's still work to do today. Here's what Jesus and I are talking about now (and you can feel free to join in the conversation):

1. Strength!

We're grateful to see improved strength and stamina, but we're asking for more and more. They say Amy has to keep the catheter until she has enough strength to take herself to the bathroom and back. Needless to say, she wants to get rid of the catheter, so I'm asking God to give her strength and muscle control to make that happen. Today maybe? That would be nice!

2. Breath!

They don't want Amy to catch pneumonia, don't want fluid to pool in her lungs, so they need her lungs to come back to full ability. So I'm praying for the Rushing Wind to fill her soul and her lungs today.

3. Farts!

Yep, still need to get gas moving through the system and to get those sleepy bowels fully awake. If they don't wake up, all that liquid she swallowed this morning will just sit in her stomach, and that could cause problems. Plus, I just think it'd be nice if she could eat food again. She hasn't eaten anything for three days now. I think it's about time to end that fast.

4. Out of the ICU?

This is more for me than for Amy because she keeps saying she wants to be able to see visitors...then she conks out, exhausted from saying she wants to see visitors. So I am still enforcing the no visitors rule until she's out of the ICU. And yes, the rumors are true. I kicked my own son out of here yesterday when she wore out from seeing him—about five minutes into his visit. And yes, when the church elders came over to pray, I blocked the door and moved them into the hallway to make their requests known unto God. (I did let them anoint me with oil as Amy's representative though!) The point is, Amy misses each and every one of you, so let's get her out of the ICU so she can start seeing you all again (in five-minute doses).

5. Gratefulness

Yes, this is a difficult time for Amy, but we are seeing God's hand and feeling his comfort in many ways. One thing I've learned is that the entire Christian life is an expression of gratefulness; we love because he first loved us. And in this situation, we are overwhelmed by the generosity of his constant, expressive love for Amy. For this we are grateful.

We love you! Amy says that today she will dedicate her flatulence to the sanctity of your friendship. (Don't you feel special now?)

Ready...set...pray!

Later...

OK, we are trying the pain test again! They've turned off the epidural and given her a higher dose of oral pain medicine. If she can stomach the oral pain medicine, and if it makes her pain tolerable this time, they will consider removing the epidural. Amy wants the epidural out because they won't let her out of the ICU as long as it's in.

Ready...set...pray!

Later...

Amy is in a lot of pain right now. She is asking for her loved ones to pray again!

Later...

OK, Amy is finally sleeping again—and sleeping hard. Our girl's had kind of a rough afternoon today, and pain management has become a significant issue. She tried twice to switch from the fentanyl drip to oral pain medicine, and the second attempt was particularly harsh for her. Earlier this morning, she was enthusiastic about getting rid of the epidural. Now she is scared about losing its security and relief.

The plan is for her to sleep one more night with the epidural in and then cold-turkey it out tomorrow with oral pain medications replacing it. The oral pain meds so far have seemed to have little effect, so please pray that her body will be strengthened by a peaceful night of sleep and that she'll be able to withstand the pain trial in store for her tomorrow.

We love you!

Later...

(From Amy!)

Awake for a few minutes. Always so tired. Thank you all so much for praying. It was rough trying to switch medications this afternoon. They'll start trying again tomorrow at 4:00 a.m. I am trying to be brave, but the pain is incredible.

The staff here at McKee has been kind, and I'm grateful.

In the TMI department…I still am not passing gas, and it's important that I do. Keep praying for farts!

Saturday, August 22, 2015

Sorry for the silence this morning—will give the full update a little later. For now, thanking God for two people: Colleen (just seeing your face brought tears to my eyes this morning!) and Erik Brolsma (be sure to get me a stud quarterback in my fantasy draft, Coach!).[5] Love to you all!

Later…

Just a quick update. Amy is resting peacefully. They are trying to gently wean her from the epidural medicine instead of going cold turkey, and that seems to be much less stressful for Amy. She's going to have to endure some amount of pain to recover, but at least now she is easing into it instead of diving right in.

She has slept most of the day since I got here, and she still tires out quickly. She misses everybody! I keep telling her that when she's stronger you will all come visit. She understands but wants you to know that she loves you all and misses you.

They put her back on oxygen because her lungs are still not strong enough, but that's just a temporary thing. She's being a good patient and doing all the exercises they tell her to do. She's tough; she's going to make it through this. It's just taking a little longer than she'd hoped.

Pain management and bowel activity are still our two main prayers right now, so keep the heavenly conversation going.

---

5. Erik is my brother-in-law and my official fantasy football talent scout.

We love you all!

P.S. Next time you take a dump, be sure to thank God for keeping your bowels awake and in tune!

Later...

Praise God for *The Big Bang Theory*! It kept Amy distracted from her pain long enough for the pain medicine to kick in. Now she's sleeping again.

If any of you were thinking of sending flowers, may I suggest an iTunes gift card instead? We've only got one season of *Big Bang Theory* on Amy's iPad.

Love you all! Thank you for praying!

Later...

Been an eventful morning! Here's what we're talking with Jesus about today:

1. Pain management

Well, apparently it hurts to have your stomach cut open and your internal organs ripped out. Who knew? The third attempt to dry up the epidural and switch to oral pain medication was a colossal failure—just too painful for our girl. Thankfully, our dear friend (and nurse) Colleen was with Amy for this third attempt, and she was truly a godsend. Amy said just having Colleen here gave her peace and comfort when she was afraid. So we're thanking God for Colleen right now!

At any rate, they were unable to remove the epidural today, so Amy is still in the isolation room of the ICU. This is discouraging for Amy, and she says, "I didn't realize how much it would really hurt." Both the doctor and the anesthesiologist came by today, and they've decided to leave in the epidural one more day but are cutting the fentanyl dosage in half to try easing Amy out of dependence on it. They are also giving her 12-hour and 4-hour oral pain medicines. She is comfortable now, but it was a rough morning, starting around 4:00.

She is also dealing with some nausea, but we don't know if that's because of the oral pain medicine, or simply anxiety, or because her bowel is still not fully functioning. At any rate, pain management has jumped to the top of our prayer list. We need to get Amy off the epidural, and she wants to get off it (so she can get out of the ICU), but it's proving more difficult than we'd hoped it would be.

2. Gassy goals

Things are happening down there in the bowel (yay!), but still no gas. This is causing the bowel to swell some, which adds to Amy's pain. They are adding Reglan to her IV in hopes that it will get her bowels moving, and (TMI alert!) they've also been doing suppositories to try to help things along. Amy has been able to process liquids, though, so that's been good. But we're still praying for loosening bowels and a little intestinal perfume. That would be a big relief for Amy, so keep up the good prayers.

3. Abdominal fluid buildup

The cancer left behind is, once again, causing fluid to build up in Amy's abdomen. The doctor says the chemotherapy is the only permanent treatment for that, but until then the only thing they can do is drain the fluid periodically. (They call it a "tap." Medical people are so weird.) Needless to say, right now is not a great time for a tap, but the cancer isn't listening to our arguments in that debate. Anyway, she still has a few more days (maybe longer) before a tap will be needed, but that's a complication we'll have to deal with sooner or later.

4. Strength!

Amy is still so weak and wears out so quickly. We need the Holy Spirit's power to strengthen her body and buoy her soul!

Again, sorry for the delay in getting this update to you. As you can guess, it's been a complicated morning. We are so grateful for every one of you—for your care, concern, and prayers. Amy says she "needs her people" and is grateful you are all here to support her in this fight.

We love you!

Sunday, August 23, 2015

Hi, all,

Have to say, everything feels better after spending a Sunday morning with Andraé Crouch and John P. Kee.[6] Ahh. Anyway, here's how the conversation with Christ is going today…

1. There's a wind blowin'!

OK, true, it's not much, but it is something! Is it coincidence that we finally see progress in this area at the same time when thousands of people in dozens of Sunday-morning congregations are praying for Amy? I think not. God certainly knows how to get glory from the most unusual things, I guess. (Somebody say amen!)

2. Kicking pain's a—

Mandi, honey, it's for you that I didn't spell out that whole word above (see how much I love you?)—but we all know what I mean. We have finally experimented our way to a successful pain management regimen, at least for now. First a 12-hour pain med, supplemented by a 4-hour additional pain med as needed. But Amy is now able to take all her pain medicines orally and—thank you, Jesus!—she is not nauseated by them (a big deal!). So, you guessed it, they successfully removed the epidural this morning, and Amy's

---

6. Yeah, I'm a gospel music fan. Isn't everybody?

pain is still at a tolerable level. Whew! Thank you so much for all your prayers! This was a difficult milestone to reach, and we felt your support the entire way. In more practical terms, this also means that as soon as she is strong enough, Amy can finally be transferred to a regular room. From there it's only a matter of time until she can come home. Also, it means we can manage her pain while she's at home and help her recovery progress to the point where she can get busy kicking chemotherapy's…um, general posterior region.

3. Abdominal fluid buildup

This is still an issue, but I guess two out of three isn't bad. As I mentioned yesterday, the cancer still inside her is once again causing fluid to build up in Amy's abdomen. The good news is that the doctor did an ultrasound today and said there's still time before a tap will be needed, so at least we are able to postpone that.

Amy is also retaining lots of water, and her IV is still pumping fluid, which she says makes her feel puffy. She was annoyed this morning because they weighed her, and all that fluid from all those sources and all that water retention has made her gain weight even though she hasn't really eaten anything in about a week. If you know anything about Amy, she's positively militaristic about her weight, so she was kind of mad. But it was also kind of good to see her have enough energy to be mad about something, so I'll take what I can get. She knows the weight will come off again down the road. Anyway, please keep praying about the abdominal fluid buildup. That's the serious problem that will have to be dealt with sooner or later.

4. Strength!

This is also a persistent concern, as Amy's strength wanes so quickly. Of course, she's been through a lot, and her body needs the rest it is demanding, but she is still weak. We need her body to get stronger so she can move forward in beating this problem—and so she can come home, where she has every season of *The Big Bang Theory* on DVD!

All right, now you know everything I know. In case we haven't mentioned it, we love you all and are so grateful to have you nearby as we work through this situation.

Also, special thanks to Erik Brolsma for handling my fantasy football draft yesterday and getting me both Drew Brees and DeMarco Murray. I smell a championship coming...

We love you!

P.S. Amy loved opening a raft of get-well cards today! Thank you for caring!

Later...

Whoa...what is that smell?

The smell of glory and answered prayers!

(If you don't know what this means, you haven't been paying attention. If you do know, then plug your nose and pray for more!)

Later...

(From Amy!)

Hey, friends! On a short break between naps...lots of groggy moments but am thankful for every bit of progress. I'm out of ICU, which means improvement. I did love the nurses and certified nursing assistants (CNAs) there though. So very kind. Got more needles and tubes removed. Down to just IV. Was able to get a short shower and am grateful to Colleen for assisting me with that and making me comfy. Hope and joy are all around! Love you all!

Later...

Well, our girl is exhausted but resting comfortably in her new room. That's right—she's finally out of the ICU! She's still struggling with an uncooperative bowel and trying to stay ahead of the pain, so keep praying about those things, but we are encouraged that she was finally strong enough to get moved down here to steerage.

She is still very weak, though, and tires out really fast. Also, they had to add a potassium IV, which burns as it goes into her arm. So as you're praying tonight, please ask God to grant relief in Amy's bowels, to strengthen her physically so she can go home, and to correct the potassium deficiency so she doesn't have to keep that fiery IV going.

Thanks! We love you!

Monday, August 24, 2015

Hi, all,

Sorry for my delinquency today—was kind of a rough morning, but Amy is doing better now. Let's see if I can catch you up without boring you silly. I'll leave out the part about when Amy acquired superpowers due to a radioactive spider bite and move on to the more interesting things.

It's been a "two steps forward, one step back" kind of morning. During the night, our girl was sleeping so peacefully that the nurse didn't want to wake her up when it was time for more Percocet. So Amy missed a dose in the cycle, and when she woke up she was in great pain. As you know, it's easier to stay ahead of pain than to try catching up to it, so it took a few hours before they were able to get that under control again. I have now begun the practice of writing (in large numbers) the exact time when Amy's next pain dose is due on the big whiteboard in her room. We haven't missed any doses since then.

Additionally, the ascites[7] in Amy's abdomen are increasing, and that,

---

7. What the good doctors here call the unwanted abdominal fluid in Amy's body.

combined with bowel swelling and lots of fluid retention in her tissue (she can barely bend her knees now), is causing constant discomfort for her. Right now we could really use a good…tempest of productive waste evacuation from the bowel. (Love you, Mandi Nappa!) That would relieve a lot of pressure on Amy's insides. Additionally, all the fluid and swelling are putting pressure on her lungs. This makes it hard for her to take deep breaths, which increases the risk of fluid in the lungs and/or pneumonia. No biggie, right?

Meanwhile, Amy is being a good patient. The surgeon/oncologist came in today and gently suggested that Amy should stop pushing herself so hard, that she doesn't have to be an overachiever. She counseled a little more rest, a little less ambition, and a little more patience. Amy seems to have taken that advice to heart.

On the bright side, Amy ate cream of chicken soup today! Yay! It's the first solid (well, sort of solid) food she's had in a week. And if she's up to it, she can splurge later and get a bowl of mashed potatoes from the cafeteria. How's that for American decadence? Also, they are cautiously optimistic that Amy will be able to come home tomorrow. (She is ready to come home, if only to get away from that IV needle in her arm and the nighttime blood draws, when they wake her up regardless of how peacefully she's sleeping.)

On the other side, Amy's strength seems to be waning each day instead of increasing, which is a concern for me. I am hopeful that the doctor's advice to rest more and let her body do the healing for her will bear fruit in this area. I've loaded up more *Big Bang Theory* episodes to help her relax, but in the irony of this situation, she's been too tired to watch them yet today. Maybe later, Sheldon. She's listening to James Taylor while she sleeps instead.

Anyway, that's where we are today. Two steps forward, with the occasional one step back. We're in it for the long haul though, so we know there'll be some bad days mixed in with many good ones to come.

Now I should go before Amy wakes up and starts practicing her web-shooting skills again. (It makes such a mess, and the nurses say web cleanup is not in their contract, so guess who gets stuck scrubbing steel-strength gossamer off the walls? I know—I'm exhausted just looking at it!)

Love you all! Thanks for taking this wild ride with us!

P.S. Amy is sleeping…but I'm pretty sure I just heard a toot! Praise Jesus! Let it rain, Lord, let it rain!

Later…

Here's some good news: Amy has had a bit of "relief," if you know what I mean. (And if you don't know, then what have you been reading for the past six days?) Anyway, we're still praying for more to come, but we're all "relieved" for little blessings!

Still cracks me up how God chooses to receive his glory. He's so much humbler about being great than I would ever be.

Tuesday, August 25, 2015

Hi, all,

Better morning today than yesterday, though today we are dealing with some nausea, which can be dangerous for someone who's just had abdominal surgery. Still, thanks to God's goodness (and your prayers), we are seeing some success in the bathroom. Hallelujah!

Spoke to Dr. Rubatt this morning, and she thinks Amy is ready to come home. We are ready for her to come home too! Today is Amy's mother's birthday, so you can bet we're squeezing all we can out of that, as we didn't get her a present. "Oh, Winnie, see how much we love you? We specifically arranged it so that the random day Amy gets to come home is on your birthday!

Now, Cinderella...I mean, Winnie...make that soup! Give that shot! Sleep at our house so you can wake up at all times of the night to help Amy while Mike snores contentedly downstairs!" Yeah, we're not the best at birthday shopping.

Amy still teeters on a tightrope of pain management, but it seems as if she does OK as long as we don't delay the timing of her medicines. Kaiser doesn't cover the prescription for her main pain medicine, and I started to complain about it. Then I realized they are spending close to $100,000 on this surgery and hospital stay and such, not counting the upcoming chemotherapy and whatever else is ahead, so I kept my mouth shut and let my credit card do the talking.

Frankenbelly (as I've taken to calling the giant scar down Amy's front) is healing nicely—no infection or other complications. We expect to have the staples removed in a week or so. Yay!

Once Amy is home, we will have a few weeks to build up her strength to get her ready for chemotherapy. They are hopeful to start by October. She will have a permanent port put in to administer the chemotherapy, which is not exciting, but that's a problem for Future Amy. Right now we just want to get her home, settled, and on the road to recovery.

She is still very weak and still tires out quickly but is looking forward to being able to see visitors at home. My only request is that you check in with me before coming over so I can try to keep her from being overwhelmed with too many people at once. But she is very much looking forward to seeing you all again, and as she gets stronger over the next few weeks, she'll be able to spend more time hosting guests. So don't forget about us three weeks from now when our lives are boring again!

Thank you for your continued love, support, and prayers. We love you!

Later...

(From Amy!)

My dear friends! I am home! I am incredibly exhausted but have found a few ways to get comfy and have had a shower (a blessing itself!) and a few bites of frozen yogurt. My mom will spend tonight here and Dad will be here tomorrow night so that Mike will get off to a good start with my recovery. I will share more tomorrow, but tonight I must sleep-sleep-sleep. I love you all! Coming home to cards and many other fun gifts is awesome!

Wednesday, August 26, 2015

(From Amy!)

Hello, my friends. One day at home. Mike and my parents have a chart for all my medicines and are working to make sure I get rest and move as much as my tired body can. I gained more than 20 pounds of water weight in my arms and legs and am moving when I can to help that go away.

It is all so slow, and I am weary. But notes and cards and silly things are making their way to me with laughter and Scripture and encouragement. Means more than I can say. Thank you. Now back to my next nap...

Thursday, August 27, 2015

Hi, loved ones!

Well, yesterday was a...um...male heir of a female dog. We are grateful for Norm and Winnie Wakefield[8] though—true examples of Jesus's care and

---

8. Amy's parents.

compassion. Things are going better today. Amy is finally eating again, and she can get up and move around a little.

We so appreciate your prayers and the many, many gifts and expressions of love toward her. We couldn't do this without you. Will try to update more later today.

We love you!

Later...

Here's what we're talking about with Jesus today:

1. Strength

Amy is finally eating again, which is a pretty big deal because it's helping her get a little more strength. The key was getting a new nausea medicine that allows her to keep food in her stomach instead of retching at the smell of anything. She's not able to sit through an entire episode of *The Big Bang Theory* yet, but she can get up and walk around the house a bit, so we're grateful for the little progress we've seen. Please continue to ask the Lord to infuse her body with his power and strength more and more each day.

2. Pain and nausea management

The medicines Amy is taking do help in these areas—there are just so many to keep up with, especially during the night. When you can't sleep, feel free to pray about Amy's recovery and our desire for her to maintain a comfortable status while her body is trying so hard to heal.

3. Joy!

Amy is constantly buoyed by your kindness, love, and support toward her. She has taken to reading her get-well cards a second and third time, and she smiles or cries every time. Right now the cards are displayed all over the coffee table in the living room, but she's asked me to stack them all in one big pile so she can read them again, so I've got that to do yet. Bonus is that Annette[9] and I are getting treated to lots of dinners at places like Panera, Chipotle, Noodles, and even SKU Grill (yay!), so thank you for your generosity! Yum!

Amy goes back to the oncologist on Tuesday. Until then we're just trying to keep her comfortable and moving forward in recovery. We're a little nervous about the approaching weekend because it's so hard to get in touch with a doctor and our pharmacy closes, but as always we continue to trust that God has his hand in this entire situation, both in the big things (cancer!) and the small (pharmacy hours!).

"I know whom I have believed, and am convinced that he is able to guard what I have entrusted to him until that day" (2 Timothy 1:12).

Thank you for your continued love, support, and prayers. We love you!

Friday, August 28, 2015

An ode to marriage (with apologies in advance):

> Some men buy pearls for girls
>   and finest gold chit,
> I splurge on prune juice
>   to help my gal…um, make poopy in the potty.

(Sorry, we're getting kind of loopy over here.)

---

9. Annette is Amy's sister who lived with us for many years.

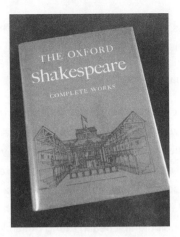

Saturday, August 29, 2015

Hi, loved ones,

Just a quick update. We had some complications during the night and into the morning, so on doctor's orders, Amy is back in the emergency room at the hospital. Will let you know more when I know more.

Thanks for your prayers!

Later...

CT scan shows some kind of bowel obstruction and air in the abdomen, so they are readmitting Amy to the hospital. Amy is resting comfortably now but is feeling discouraged about the setback. She appreciates your prayers and love though and says to tell you "Thanks so much!"

Later...

Some have asked for more information than I have been giving about Amy's current condition, so here's everything I know.

Be forewarned, this is very long and covers stuff I've talked about in the past, so feel free to skip this if you're up to date.

Question: OK, so what's going on with Amy?

Answer: As most of you know, Amy is very health conscious. She eats well, exercises five days a week at the gym, and lives a very active, healthy, and joyful life. As part of her routine body maintenance, over the past three months Amy has had an annual physical, a health screening at work, a standard preventive colonoscopy, and a life insurance physical. All those screenings indicated that Amy was in excellent health. In fact, the insurance company gave Amy their highest health rating possible and lowest annual premium available.

Then…

In early August, Amy started complaining of pain in her abdomen. She thought it was a uterine cyst or something mild. She tried to make an appointment with our family doctor (a woman), but she wasn't available. So Amy went to see the physician assistant (PA) instead. His diagnosis was that Amy was constipated, and he sent her home with advice about laxatives. She tried that, but the pain got worse, and she noticed unusual bloating in her stomach (which we later found out was fluid). Then the PA said she probably had an infection, so Amy took an antibiotic. When that also proved ineffective, they finally scheduled an ultrasound.

While waiting for the ultrasound appointment, Amy felt so much pain that she went to an urgent care facility early on August 11, 2015. They refused to see her. They said she was already under a doctor's care, so they didn't want to get involved. Amy left in tears but waited it out anyway.

Finally, on August 12, she had an ultrasound that revealed ascites (large amounts of fluid pooled in her abdomen). Ascites are normally caused by liver damage, so they assumed alcoholism. We politely explained that alcoholism wasn't the cause because Amy doesn't drink. So they sent her to the hospital for a CT scan.

That scan revealed numerous tumors in Amy's abdomen and ovaries, including one that was more than seven inches long and stretched from side to side across Amy's stomach, attached to her bowel. The PA (thankfully) disappeared. Our family doctor took over and immediately scheduled Amy to see Dr. Jennifer Rubatt, a gynecological oncologist / surgeon here in Loveland (one of the top in the state!), and sent the test results to the oncologist. Dr. Rubatt looked at the test results and immediately scheduled Amy for surgery, sight unseen, on August 19.

So within two weeks, Amy went from being told she was in near-perfect health to being told she had aggressive cancer that required an immediate operation.

Question: What kind of cancer are we talking about?

Answer: Our oncologist confirmed that the cancer began in Amy's uterus and spread to her ovaries and into her peritoneal (abdominal) cavity. So basically it can be called uterine cancer or ovarian cancer or peritoneal cancer. Our oncologist has been calling it peritoneal cancer as kind of a catchall phrase, and she says these kinds of cancers all are given the same treatment. So we can call it whatever we want; the result is the same. Surgery to remove the tumors followed by chemotherapy.

Question: How serious is this?

Answer: According to our oncologist, Amy's is stage III-C cancer, which is near the top of the scale. (Stage IV cancer is the worst.)[10] Livestrong.org says, "According to the American Cancer Society, those with stage III-C have a 35 percent chance of living for 5 years after diagnosis." So yeah, this could be the thing that kills our girl. Or not. We'll have to wait and see how God

---

10. Again, we found out later that Amy's cancer was actually stage IV-B. We knew it was bad—just didn't know how bad.

chooses to work in this situation. According to our oncologist, Amy seems the type to beat the odds because (a) she's relatively young, (b) she's otherwise in very good health, and (c) cancer research has continued to progress, even in the past five years.

Question: So how did the surgery go?

Answer: Amy had surgery to remove the tumors on August 19. That included a full hysterectomy (removal of uterus and ovaries) as well as removal of the appendix. Our MMA-style surgeon also peeled that large tumor off her bowel by hand (eww—and so cool!), which meant they could leave Amy's bowel intact (an answer to prayer!). However, there were just too many smaller tumors, and they couldn't remove them without permanently damaging Amy's internal organs. The oncologist said it looked like someone had sneezed tiny tumors all over Amy's bowel. She had to leave them in. That also meant she couldn't put in a localized port to direct the chemotherapy treatments, which would have been easier on Amy and more effective in treatment. Instead she will have to do intravenous treatments.

Question: And after the surgery?

Answer: That's where we are now. Amy is still trying to recover from the trauma of the operation. I've taken to (affectionately) calling her Frankenbelly because she has a large scar that runs from the bottom of her sternum all the way down to her bathing suit line. The scar is healing wonderfully—apparently our oncologist is an artist. No infection, clean incision, looks really good. It's what's inside that's causing our girl problems.

Amy's bowel has never fully recovered from the surgery. We had enough progress to go home for a few days but had to be readmitted to the hospital today. There is some kind of blockage in her intestines. This has basically shut down the bottom portion of her bowels, causing her a lot of pain and discomfort and forcing fluid (bile and acid) to pool in Amy's stomach. Plus there is air trapped in her abdomen (outside the stomach) and ascites forming in there again. A little civil war inside her gut, generally speaking.

Question: So what's going on now?

Answer: We are in the hospital. They've put a tube down Amy's nose to drain the excess fluid in her stomach (a huge help, but Amy hates the tube because it is very uncomfortable). Amy is still very weak, and they are trying to get her strong enough to start chemotherapy. The oncologist expects Amy to be hospitalized until the middle of next week and even canceled her office appointment on Tuesday. (By the way, we were grateful to see our oncologist come in and sit with Amy awhile today, on her day off. It was almost funny to see how the ER staff jumped into action when Dr. Rubatt walked into the room. But that's a story for another day.)

Amy struggles constantly with pain management, weakness, and nausea. Plus she was very discouraged to have to go back into the hospital after thinking she was making progress toward recovery. When you are praying for our wonderful Frankenbelly, feel free to mention those things to Jesus during your conversation.

Question: What are the next steps?

Answer: First, get Amy's bowels working again—something that has become a long, difficult process up to this point. Next, complete the physical recovery from the surgery. Somewhere in there, it'll probably be good to get some professional counseling as well, just to begin processing all the mixed-up emotions being forced on Amy in this time. Then, ideally by the beginning of October, start chemotherapy. From there, who knows what? We'll have to take this adventure as it comes to us.

Question: How's Amy handling all this?

Answer: She's working through the onslaught of pain and emotion as you might expect. Some good days, some bad days. Plenty of Scripture, James Taylor, *The Big Bang Theory*, and repeated viewings of *Pride and Prejudice*.

Amy has pretty much no fear of death though. She says if this is the end, she's ready because she knows who waits for her after that. If it's not the end, she'll keep fighting as long as Jesus gives her strength to do so. What scares her is the trauma of the treatment necessary to save her life. Surgery was fearful, but she marched into that operating room anyway. She continues to feel anxiety about all the pains associated with recovery. She's afraid of the awfulness associated with chemotherapy, the prospect that she might require more surgeries in the future, the possibility of serious permanent disabilities, and all the unknowns that come just from having cancer.

Despite the fear and pain, she moves forward and grits her teeth and endures and prays and trusts in God. This is something unique, I think. Many people begin to doubt God or castigate him when enduring sudden or severe hardship, but she doesn't think like that. She dealt with this issue years ago, I guess, and now, when life isn't to her liking, she doesn't wag a finger God's way. She shrugs and says what Simon Peter said when asked if he would abandon Jesus because so many others had: "To whom shall [I] go? You [Jesus] have the words of eternal life" (John 6:68). He is God regardless of what we want or expect of him, and he will continue to be God when we are happy with his tender grace toward us as well as when we are disappointed and angry at the seeming harshness of his grace. He is always God, and we will always trust him. We understand why Job could say with such conviction, "Though he slay me, yet will I hope in him" (Job 13:15). He's earned that from us in more ways than we could ever describe.

Question: What if I have more questions?

Answer: Honestly, now you know as much as I do. If you have new questions—especially questions about cancer or treatment or doctors or hospitals or whatever—chances are very good my answer will be "I don't know." And please don't be offended at me when I inevitably fail to give you all you want to know, or fail to provide enough updates, or just don't do a good enough job as the unexpected chronicler of Amy's unexpected illness. It's just that sometimes I have trouble keeping up with everything happening around me, so chalk it up to my ineptitude and keep walking with us through this anyway. I'll try to do better for you, I promise. Also, feel free to look up anything you want online. Here at Nappaland, we are all just learning as we go.

Question: Any last thoughts?

Answer: Amy has been genuinely humbled and grateful for the outpouring of love and support you've shown her. She's lived a life worthwhile, and you are proof of that. Please continue your prayers in the long days ahead. As her battle and recovery drag from days into weeks into months into years, many of you could easily forget the passion you feel for her right now—and of course, that would be natural. We hold no ill will about that. Instead, we've decided to bask in your grace and love and prayers for as long as you want to give them to us. You've already given us more than we deserve.

Thank you so much for your many kindnesses to Amy and to our family. As always,

WE LOVE YOU!

Sunday, August 30, 2015

Hi, everyone,

Just a short update. We've seen some progress today! Amy is still weak, and the tube down her throat continues to make her miserable. But the tube is doing its job, and we've seen some signs of her bowels coming back to life, so this is a big relief. The doctor says she wants to avoid having to do a second surgery, so they're trying a consistent, conservative approach for a few more days. We were very grateful when Amy finally had some bowel activity today! Please keep praying—we feel your love.

Monday, August 31, 2015

Hi, all,

Here's where we are today so far:

Amy is exhausted but feeling much better than she did yesterday. She didn't sleep well (hence the exhaustion), but her pain level is lower, and we're seeing consistent progress in reactivating her bowel. That alone has given her a lot of pain relief—so we're still thanking Jesus for poop!

They did the CT scan this morning and kept her in there more than an hour. They appeared to want to be very thorough and patient as they conducted the scan, so we're grateful for that. We have not heard what the results of the scan are but hope to hear before day's end.

Amy is more alert and in better spirits today. For some reason, having less pain makes her more relaxed and communicative—she's so weird. If not for the uncomfortable (and kind of disgusting) tube down her nose, she'd probably be able to take visitors. Maybe tomorrow. I'll let you know.

Anyway, that's where we are at this point. If you have questions, feel free to send them to Amy's personal assistant: bill.gates@microsoft.com.

We love you all!

Later...

(From Amy!)

Huge thanksgiving. I just got the tube out of my nose, so I can talk again! Enjoying a Popsicle. Have to stay another night, but I am free of the nose tube that was tormenting me. Yes, I know it was helping me too...

Tuesday, September 1, 2015

Hi, loved ones,

Good news to report today! Our girl made good progress yesterday and is starting to look more like herself again. I think, though, that they may have accidentally removed her sense of humor during the surgery. For the past two days, I've been throwing out extremely funny jokes (even added a Liz Lemon dance move for sauce), and all she does is roll her eyes at me. Hmm. I'll have to make a note to talk to the doctor about that.

Anyway, things are not normal yet but definitely improving. The CT scan shows that although Amy's bowel is still swollen some, it is less swollen than it was on Saturday, and (here's the really good news) the blockage that was causing her so much discomfort has cleared. Yay, God! Thank you, Jesus! There is still air in her abdomen, but less air, and the doctor thinks that what is there will be reabsorbed into Amy's system without any problem. Same for fluid in the abdomen (although we will eventually have to deal with the ascites). There was concern about a possible contagious bowel infection—they put Amy on isolation and all the nurses had to wear gloves and such to even enter the room—but tests for that came back negative. So all in all, a good day yesterday.

They also removed the nose tube yesterday, and Amy just about did her own Liz Lemon dance over that. She's been steadily improving since.

We had hoped for a return home today, but the doctor wants to keep her in the hospital one more day just to make sure Amy doesn't relapse again. They are having her try "real" food and watching to see if that causes any problems. So far so good. (Pray that things keep moving through without incident!)

Just now they've finally removed all the tubes and IV and stuff attached to various parts of Amy's body, so our girl is free to roam about the hospital room. And of course, now that she finally has complete freedom to move, she promptly went to sleep. As the guy from the *Pirates of the Caribbean* might say, "Now that's what you call ironic."

Amy's progress also means she's taking visitors today, so if you want to drop by, message me to let me know when (so I can try to coordinate visits so Amy doesn't get overwhelmed). She's still kind of weak and wears out quickly, but she'd love to see you, so let me know if you want to come by.

We are grateful for the recent evidence of God's healing hand and continue to be confident that "he is able to guard what I have entrusted to him until that day" (2 Timothy 1:12).

We love you!

Wednesday, September 2, 2015

Hi, all,

Sorry for the delay in updating today—been busy, but a good kind of busy. Amy is officially home and resting again! She's in much better shape this time around, off the narcotic pain medicines and able to eat at last. Yay! Thank you, Jesus! She came home around 11:00-ish this morning, ate some chocolate ice cream and some soup, and then took a long nap. Now she's watching the classic film *Bringing Up Baby* and trying to relax.

Amy has two weeks to build up her strength before being reevaluated by her doctor. We lost about a week in the schedule, thanks to our most recent hospital vacation, so they're still trying to work out when chemotherapy will begin. They want to start as soon as possible, but Amy is just not strong enough yet. She lost about 10 percent of her normal body weight since just last Saturday, and she wasn't a big girl to begin with. We're supposed to fill her up on protein and dairy (yes, they specifically included "ice cream" in the dairy prescription!), so we're trying to do that. She's definitely eating better but still only able to stomach small servings. We're working on fattening her up. We'll know more about whether she can handle chemotherapy in two weeks.

If you think of it, please pray for Amy's sister Annette (who is developmentally disabled and lives with us). Annette stayed home from work today. She said she was so worried about Amy that she felt sick to her stomach and couldn't sleep. So the first thing Amy did when she got home (even before we brought in her bag from the hospital) was sit on Annette's bed and spend a few minutes reassuring and encouraging her. Annette finally went to sleep soon after and seems to be doing better this afternoon. Anyway, if you know Annette, and if you think about it, please lift her up in your prayers too.

I think that's it for the moment! Now that we're home and trying to get into some semblance of a routine, I may not update as often, so please don't be frustrated with me. I'm still trying to figure out the rules of this whole "Hey, my wife has crazy cancer and a million friends and family who love her" thing. I'll try to update at least once a day.

She's doing really well and is able to take visitors in short bursts as long as we make sure to give her a little recovery time between visits. If you want to come by and say "Hey, Amy!" just message me to let me know, and we'll work out a good time for you to see her. She loves you all and misses you very much! Thank you for all your love and support and prayers!

Thursday, September 3, 2015

Hi, loved ones,

OK, here's the story for today. Amy woke up about 2:30 in the morning with abdominal pain and bowel discomfort. She took pain medicine but still struggled. She felt like it would help if she could, um, activate her insides, but she tried and wasn't able to. So she tried to go back to sleep but only slept fitfully.

Around 7:30 this morning, Amy's mother was sitting in our living room when she saw several cars and trucks pull up outside our house. Five older men got out of their cars and walked up into our driveway. Then with hands outstretched, they paused to pray awhile over our house. When they were done, they quietly got back into their vehicles and drove away.

About 15 minutes later, Amy woke up with "the urge." Success! She finally felt relief from the pain and was able to drop back into a restful sleep. She's felt fine the rest of this morning.

So that's what's going on today. We're still thanking God for prayers and for poop! We love you and are so grateful for your support. And if you were one of the men who came by this morning, thanks for your kindness (and for not waking us up!).

Friday, September 4, 2015

Hi, all,

Quiet morning over here in Nappaland today—it's been a while since I've been able to say that! Amy is doing fairly well. She still has some trouble with occasional pain flare-ups and bowel discomfort (usually during the night), but we are definitely seeing improvement in both those areas. We feel your prayers and kindnesses every day.

Amy has taken to walking around the perimeter of the backyard to help move forward her recovery. Yesterday she scared a little cottontail rabbit hiding in the bushes, and the dog (our five-pound Chihuahua) seemed to like that. At first the dog would follow her around the yard, but now he just sits in the grass and watches her with a bemused look on his face that appears to say, "People be crazy."

Special thanks today goes to Joani Schultz[11] for making Amy laugh yesterday. Joani gave Amy a jar full of "Reasons why Amy brings me joy." Yesterday's reason was "Because you threw up on me" during an airplane ride. (Yeah, long story, and apparently weird things bring Joani joy, but it made Amy laugh, so I'm all for it.) We love you, Joani!

Today I really should be working on my next novel (OK, well, starting my next novel. OK, at least thinking about starting my next novel), but the siren living in the guest room upstairs has lured me away from my work with melodies that promise a *Back to the Future* marathon, so what can I do? Sometimes you just have to save the clock tower. (But don't tell my editor—she thinks I'm right on schedule to meet my deadline…yikes!)

Prayers for today include strength (always a big one—we've got to get our girl strong enough to face chemotherapy, which looms), full bowel healing and consistent bowel function, pain management, and, you know, that someday soon I might actually start working on that elusive novel.

We love you all!

Later…

OK, so we made it only about 45 minutes into *Back to the Future* before my siren fell asleep, but it was definitely the best 45 minutes of my day. Sure hope Marty and Doc are able to get out of their little time-travel predicament without us.

---

11. Joani Schultz is CCO at Group Publishing. For many years she worked closely with Amy there. Apparently during one of their work/play trips together, Amy threw up and some of it got on Joani. Surprisingly, Amy didn't get fired. In fact, Amy and Joani remained fast friends and dedicated coworkers until the very end.

Saturday, September 5, 2015

(From Amy!)

Hi, everyone! I am feeling a tiny bit more energetic (only one nap so far instead of three), and the nurse who stopped by said I'm doing well. I really need to gain some weight and strength, so please be praying for that.

I have been incredibly encouraged by your prayers and notes. Thank you, thank you, thank you!

Sunday, September 6, 2015

(From Amy!)

Good morning, dear friends. As you head out to worship today, please keep me in your prayers and invite others to pray as well.

- Strength and weight gain.
- There's still a lot of cancer in my body. Healing, whether through a miracle or through medicine.
- He won't admit it, but this is taking a toll on Mike. Strength for him is needed.

This is our chance to shine for Jesus! Shine bright today!

I love you all!

Wednesday, September 9, 2015

Hi, loved ones,

Here's how the conversation with Christ is going today:

1. **Wow, thanks so much for returning function to Amy's bowels, for keeping her spirits up, and for all the love and care and concern and kindness being lavished on our family right now.** It's an eye-opening experience to have a front-row seat to this moment where grace and sorrow seem to be holding hands like lovers. We're aware of your presence in the storm and discovering your joy in unexpectedly intimate ways.

2. **Amy is still weak—you know this already.** Still, it helps to talk about it. She's still losing weight, down to 106 pounds, and her little frame feels more like bone than flesh right now. She gives great hugs though. There's love in those arms that seems stronger and more permanent than any physical weakness. She's doing her "homework" too...eating the right foods, drinking that protein, juicing and smoothie-ing as much as she can take. She's got very little appetite, though, so it's kind of a chore for her just to eat or to walk around the backyard. We want our girl to grow strong again, but progress is slow in this area. We continue to ask for your Holy Spirit to invade and strengthen Amy's blood and bones and body and bowel. Power is your domain, and we want her to live in that place with you. We want to be there too.

3. **Time is always on our minds but out of our grasp.** We leave that in your hands, where it belongs.

4. **Chemotherapy looms like a bully.** No, like a drill sergeant...well, maybe like a good friend who's determined to tough-love us into more than we think is possible—in ways we don't want to endure. Regardless, it waits, and only you can make it more than just an awful medical procedure. So get us ready for that and hold our hands as we walk through it. We know you will.

5. **Give us rest.** We're feeling tired, Lord, and we're still just at the beginning. Teach us rest, and we'll try to learn the lesson well. We love you, Jesus, and are grateful too. You do all things well, and we see that magnified in Amy. Amen.

And we love you too, loved ones! Thank you for standing with us in the gaps of prayer.

Saturday, September 12, 2015

(From Amy!)

Hey, everyone. Back in the hospital with ab pain. May be another blockage. So once again…praying for bowel movement! You know how to pray!

Later…

Hi, loved ones.

OK, sorry for the delay in reporting. Amy got very sick in the night and, as many of you know, nighttime is kryptonite for my own chronic illness,[12] so I was fairly useless to help her (or to post at length on Facebook or to answer texts and emails with concerned questions about Amy's condition). Sorry! Thankfully, Amy's dad, Norm Wakefield, came over around 3:30 a.m. and rushed her to the hospital. (Rumor is he even ran a few red lights!)

Anyway, there is another bowel blockage causing Amy significant abdominal pain and prompting bouts of vomiting. They've got her on pain medicine and nausea medicine now, so she's finally resting comfortably. The hope is that the blockage will work itself out over the next 24 hours. If she hasn't had a bowel movement by morning, the dreaded nose tube goes in again, so Amy really wants your prayers about that.

The timing is bad for this because, believe it or not, Amy's oncologist is in Wisconsin getting married today. Still, even though we wish she were here, we hope she hears nothing of this until after she gets back from her mini honeymoon. During Amy's surgery, Dr. Rubatt was assisted by another

---

12. I have a condition called chronic gastritis, which basically means I have frequent nausea. It was the result of a gallbladder surgery I had when I was 33, after which I didn't heal correctly, which in turn damaged the inside of my stomach, and that developed into chronic gastritis. To treat it, I take medicine every two hours (to coat my stomach) and eat a low-fat diet. That treatment is generally effective, but during the night my stomach empties out and my medicine wears off. So when I wake up in the morning, I almost always feel sick to my stomach—kind of like having morning sickness for your entire life.

oncologist here in Loveland, and gratefully, he's been the one treating her in the hospital this time. He's familiar with Amy's situation, and we feel very comfortable with him.

They are telling us that this problem with repeated bowel blockage is a symptom of the cancer left inside Amy. The doctor said that all the little tumors in there are spread all over her bowels and that they are sticky, like gummy bears. When her bowels move and turn as they were created to do, the tumors on the outside of them stick to each other. That can cause a kink in the bowel (like a twist in a hose). According to the doctor, this will keep recurring until they are able to attack the tumors with chemotherapy. They want to start the chemotherapy as soon as possible but need Amy to be healthy and strong enough for it, though they may just go ahead with it and hope for the best if she keeps having this bowel obstruction problem. We'll have to wait and see how that plays out, but Amy is ready to start the chemotherapy right now.

Meanwhile, our prayers today are for (1) clearing of the bowel blockage followed by comfortable bowel movement, (2) relief from pain and suffering for Amy, (3) strength (as usual!), and (4) continued experience of God's presence in both the good and awful moments. He is always near.

Love you all!

Sunday, September 13, 2015

(From Amy!)

Hello, my dear friends! I just talked to my doctor and will be sent home today— rejoicing all around! Have to eat only super-mushy foods for a while but so thankful to be heading back home again! Thank you for your prayers. There is a good chance of this same kink happening again, so please pray that it will not recur. Love to you all!

Tuesday, September 15, 2015

Hi, loved ones,

We had another setback last night. Amy is in a lot of pain and was vomiting all night long. Trying to determine if she needs to go back to the hospital or what to do next. Thank you for your prayers!

Later…

Back to the emergency room. Will update with details when I'm able. Sorry!

Later…

Amy is in the ER. They've got her on pain and nausea medicine, and now she's sleeping—a welcome respite after last night. She started having a lot of pain and nausea yesterday evening but tried to tough it out. Even with repeated doses of Percocet and nausea medicine, she was unable to control the pain and started vomiting repeatedly. We were hoping to hold out until we could see Amy's oncologist at 3:00 p.m. today, but when we called the office this morning, the nurse told us her doctor was in surgery this morning, and after listening to Amy's symptoms, the nurse instructed me to take Amy back to the hospital ER. So that's where we are now. As an added bonus, Amy's sister Annette was also sick in the night and had to stay home from work today. I think hearing Amy being so sick nearby was just too much stress for Annette's gentle system. So be praying for peace and health for Annette today too.

We don't know what effect this latest setback will have on the chemotherapy schedule. We are hoping it's just a glitch because we really need to get started on the chemo for both health and financial reasons. We'll know more after we are able to talk to her oncologist, which we assume will be later this afternoon. For now, we are just trying to keep Amy comfortable as we wait to see what God intends to do with us today.

OK, now you know everything I know. We love you!

P.S. ER doctor just came in. They are going to do another CT scan. Will let you know the results when I know.

Later...

CT scan results show another bowel blockage, adhesions (possibly scar tissue) on her bowels, and increased fluid (ascites) pooling in her abdomen from the cancer. Looks like we'll be heading back to our regular room on the second floor for a while. I'm going to see about joining a frequent visitor club. Maybe we'll get an upgrade on ice chips for our fourth visit or something.

Later...

OK, what a day. Let's see if I can catch you up on the adventure so far.

We met with the oncologist for a good half hour or more this evening. (Her wedding was very nice. Thank you for asking.) Amy's doctor says we can't wait any longer to start the chemotherapy, so even though it isn't the optimum circumstance, she's planning to begin the treatment on Thursday while Amy is still in the hospital. (Looks like she'll be here at least until Friday or Saturday.) In deference to time and convenience, they are going to forego having a surgeon install a subcutaneous port through which to administer the chemotherapy. Instead, a nurse will install a PICC (peripherally inserted central catheter) line in her arm. Not as pretty, I guess, but it's faster and gets the job done. Meanwhile, Amy's primary task is to convince her bowels to unblock and start working again before Thursday.

The doctor confirmed that Amy will lose her hair within the next three weeks or so. Amy was disappointed but took the news with grace and without complaint. She is bummed about it though. And for the record, she doesn't want anyone to shave their heads in solidarity (though she appreciates the sentiment). She says if you want to show solidarity, wear a Mickey Mouse pin or T-shirt or something.

Once she starts chemotherapy, her immune system will be weakened, so the doctor is having her get a flu shot and a pneumonia shot ahead of time. The doctor also suggested flu shots for anyone who will be visiting Amy while she's undergoing chemotherapy. I'm getting mine tomorrow, and her parents already got theirs today. If you think you'll want to visit Amy over the next few months, please get a flu shot before coming over. Our girl is already in enough pain—having to suffer through the flu on top of chemotherapy because one of her kindhearted loved ones hugged it into her weakened system would just make her life that much more difficult.

And yes, we did ask the doctor the hard question tonight as well. She was empathetic but honest with us.

She said this disease "is going to shorten Amy's life expectancy," but she couldn't say by how much or make any predictions. She said we have to wait and see how the cancer responds to the chemotherapy treatment. She said in most women, the cancer does come back even after chemotherapy sends it into remission, that it can come back in as little as a few months or within a few years. It's rare for a woman to go five years cancer-free with an illness like Amy's. But again, we won't really know what Amy's prospects are until after we see how effective the chemotherapy is and how Christ decides to work in this situation. Not great news, I know, but take heart. Our girl is ready for whatever may come. Plus, we both agreed that regardless of what happens, we've had a great ride together. (Insert hospital-bed high-five here.)

In the end, though, our lives are neither in our own hands (no, not even in your healthy ones) nor in a doctor's hands but safely kept in the hands of the One who invented life to begin with. We continue to enjoy Christ's comfort and presence during this time and are grateful that he is using you to minister strength and health to us each day. We have many days ahead of us, I think, and we intend to enjoy them all.

I think that gives you enough for your prayer list tonight! Thank you for all you do and for who you are to Amy. We love you!

Wednesday, September 16, 2015

(From Amy!)

Good morning, wonderful friends!

I am doing well right now—with the pain medicine, I was able to sleep soundly last night and got a nice shower this morning—taking joy in the moment by moment. Waiting to hear when they will put in my PICC line. I'm not sure what that entails. Thanks for your prayers. You all are amazing, and I'm thankful!

Later...

So apparently I need a shower or something. Just got kicked out (in the nicest way) by the PICC nurse, who said she needs to sterilize Amy's room. I am not sanitary enough to stay in. Maybe I should buy new deodorant.

Anyway, they are putting the PICC line in Amy's arm right now. She's not happy about it. She hates needles and is very anxious about the process of insertion. Also, she's disappointed because the PICC line will mean more daily maintenance than the subcutaneous port. Yoga classes will be difficult, and she can't let the PICC line get wet, so no swimming, and she must always keep it wrapped in the shower. And she can't lift more than ten pounds, which will make it hard to cuddle with our granddaughter (her favorite thing). Still, she's trying to be brave and trying to keep a good attitude. We knew the port would have been better, but we can't wait any longer for that, and the PICC line will do the job we need to have done—and sooner, like tomorrow. So we are thanking God for small blessings.

Still, pray for Amy right now, as she's scared about getting the PICC installed.

We love you!

Later…

OK, PICC line is in! They couldn't get it to work on her left arm, so after four failed tries, she allowed them to switch to her right arm. Went right in with no problem.

She's doing fine now, though she's trying to get used to having this permanent thing in her right arm. Overall though, today is much better than yesterday. Amazing how your spirits cheer when pain is eliminated.

Thank you all for your love and prayers!

Later…

Amy is in good spirits. They are watching her pain levels pretty closely and acting fast to make sure they don't spike out of control again, so that's a good thing. Meanwhile, her bowel has really slowed down, which is a bad thing.

Because the chemotherapy drugs will also slow down her bowel, the doctor wants evidence that it is moving again (yes, nephew, that means farting) before starting the chemotherapy. After checking out Amy today, the oncologist made the call to postpone the first treatment until Friday.

So here's the call to prayer for today and tomorrow: "Lord of all, please gas up this hall!"

Ready…set…pray!

Thursday, September 17, 2015

(From Amy!)

Hey! A quick morning update. (1) Bowels moving and doing fine—praising God! (2) A chemo nurse will meet with me later today for a teaching session. (3) Chemo will be tomorrow, and this time they will do it in my hospital room. Things are moving along! Thanks for so much prayer and love!

Friday, September 18, 2015

Hi, loved ones,

OK, here's the update so far, and I apologize in advance because today's kind of hectic, and I don't know how much else I'll be able to post for the rest of the day. But meanwhile…

1. Amy LOVES all the Mickey love going on today. She bragged to her chemo nurse about all the pictures of people wearing Mickey Mouse stuff in solidarity with her today, so her nurse drew a big Mickey Mouse emblem on her patient board in the hospital to join in. So yeah, you guys rock.

2. They spent most of the morning giving Amy pre-chemo drugs that are supposed to help reduce some of the early symptoms of the chemotherapy. They finally started the first chemo drug (Taxol) around noon and are now monitoring her every 15 minutes to make sure she doesn't have an allergic reaction to it. This drug will drip into her system over the next three hours. After that, they'll start administering a second chemotherapy drug (carboplatin), which will take about an hour to drip in. Then we wait to see how it all affects our girl.

3. The chemotherapy nurse also talked (for two hours!) about all the side effects of these chemotherapy drugs. Wow. A lot of horrible things are possible. It was kind of like hearing the bully at school say, "Would you rather be punched in the face or in the crotch?" All the options are awful. Still, no one experiences all the side effects, and many people have only a few side effects or mild side effects, so we are asking Jesus to give us the easy way through this. (Feel free to join in that prayer!) Also, FYI, Amy is toxic for about 48 hours after a treatment, so if you come in contact with bodily fluid from her during that time (like saliva or bathroom stuff or if you clean up after she's been sick), you'll need to be sure to disinfect yourself thoroughly and wear nitrile gloves.

4. The chemotherapy nurse emphasized again how susceptible Amy will be to random infections while she's in chemotherapy, especially during days 7 through 14 after a treatment (when she is in a "nadir"[13] and most vulnerable). So even though I love you all, I will kick any of you out of my house if I hear even a sniffle or cough or if I know you've been exposed to the flu or a cold or whatever. I figure it's better to risk offending you than to risk piling illness on top of Amy's cancer-weakened body. (Plus, I'm kind of a jerk anyway, and this gives me an excuse for my antisocial behavior.)

5. We have some rough days ahead over the next six months, but Amy and I have talked about it, and we've come to the conclusion that our best days are still ahead of us, not behind us. So like the apostle Paul, "This one thing I do, forgetting those things which are behind, and reaching forth unto those things which are before, I press toward the mark for the prize of the high calling of God in Christ Jesus" (Philippians 3:13-14 KJV).

We love you! Mickey on!

---

13. "Nadir" basically means "low point." In chemo it refers to the period after a treatment when the white blood cell count is very low, which makes Amy more susceptible to infection.

Saturday, September 19, 2015

(From Amy!)

Hello, everyone! Wanted to give a quick update. Chemo day went great. No nausea or other side effects. Praise God!

The night went well too—lots of wake-ups from nurses, but I always went right back to sleep. Today I am also doing just fine. Lots to be thankful for!

Today I am on a sort of quarantine because all my fluids contain chemo. So I am not touching anyone, and others are wearing gloves to touch me or things I touch.

I am not sure when I will go home or anything like that. For the moment, I am praising God for how things have gone so far. I know the prayers of you all are carrying me in this, and I simply can't thank you enough. You are a blessing. I am grateful.

Sunday, September 20, 2015

Hi, loved ones,

Sorry for the tardiness in posting today. It's been a busy day, but mostly good. Amy is home now and in the "fatigue" cycle of the chemotherapy treatment. She is very weak and barely able to get up to go to the bathroom, but this is a sign that the chemotherapy drugs are working, so we are thankful even for this.

We are also grateful that Amy hasn't had any serious side effects so far from the treatment. Yay, God! The only thing unusual so far is that Amy had hiccups for about 24 hours after the treatment.

On the flip side, Amy's bowels have slowed down again since she came home, so it's time to pray for the fragrance of flatulence in our guest room. The sooner the better, God willing. She is still not able to eat anything other than pure liquid (not even lumpy yogurt), so that's a struggle as well. More to pray about, so you know what to do.

Last but not least, we are *extremely* grateful for our friend Ellen, who is a chemo nurse in real life and spent all day today with Amy, giving her the "Rich and Famous Private Health Care Treatment." And she and her husband, Rick, even bought me dinner to boot. *Niiice.* (If you see Rick and Ellen somewhere, be sure to hug them good and hard for us.)

Thank you all so much for your prayers. We love you!

Monday, September 21, 2015

Rough night and difficult morning so far, with abdominal swelling, nausea, and increased pain. Not sure what we're doing wrong here, but whatever we're doing, it's not working. Trying to avoid having to go back to the hospital, so you know what to do.

Ready…set…pray!

We love you!

Later…

Spoke to Dr. Rubatt. She said we're doing all the right things and to keep at it until we start seeing results. Also going into the office at 3:00 today, where they will see about maybe draining some of the ascites fluid. We'll have to wait and see about that. Meanwhile, Phenergan seems to be doing its job, and our girl is finally sleeping. Of course, now I have to wake her up to give her more medicine.

Later...

Amy was able to go to the Cancer Center and get her shot (yay!). The shot was time sensitive and will help increase her white blood cell count as she takes on the chemotherapy, so it was important to get it done. Of course, she threw up as soon as we got home—but she got the shot. We're grateful for that.

She's handling the chemotherapy very well—no abnormal side effects. The thing that's causing 90 percent of her troubles is the frequent recurrence of bowel blockages caused by the "sticky" tumors inside her abdomen. She's in a lot of bowel pain right now, which means she has to take the narcotic pain medicine, which in turn causes constipation that aggravates the bowel blockages, which causes a lot of pain and…well, you get the idea. So we're asking Christ to smooth things over in the bowels, to make things less sticky in there, and to unkink the bowels so they can function properly. Doctor says the best thing to make this stop is the chemotherapy, but it will take at least two treatments over three to five weeks to really make a difference. Meanwhile, our girl is plagued with pain and nausea, so we're trying to keep her comfortable while we march toward success.

So be sure to thank Jesus for the positive reaction to chemotherapy, but also pray for improved bowel function to get Amy through to the next treatment.

Love you all!

P.S. No visitors except immediate family right now—sorry! It's just too overwhelming for Amy. Maybe in a few days? I'll be sure to let you know. Thanks!

Later...

Wow, long day, but Amy is finally resting comfortably. Still no real progress on the bowel blockage, but we finally caught up to the pain around 8:00 p.m., which in turn seems to have relieved the nausea (though we kept her on nausea medicine for the night as a preventive step).

It's interesting sometimes when you see a mountain of an obstacle looming right in front of you, and for a while you think there must be nothing bigger than that mountain you face. You wonder what the heck you're going to do about it, because honestly, there's nothing you can do about it. Then you look a little higher, or maybe a little to the right or left, and you realize you've seen only part of the view—that your nearsighted perspective has allowed that close-up obstacle to block the sight of an even larger, more beautiful mountain range behind it, towering over it in snow-capped glory. By comparison, that little mountain you're facing is just a temporary speed bump, and with a little patience and effort, you're going to get over it and get on to the good stuff waiting behind it.

I think that's where we are today. This recurring bowel blockage seems large and insurmountable until we take time to look a little past this moment to see what lies beyond this temporary holdup.

Everyone we trust and respect keeps telling us we're doing all the right things, and we believe that's true. That means all we need to add to the equation is time. If we are faithful with God's creation (Amy's body), time will bring about the result we desire (clearing of the bowel blockage). It's an issue of perspective, a chance to focus on the larger, more inviting mountain of refuge that sits comfortably beyond this moment. If we wait this out, this harsh time will become only a memory we wave at in our rearview mirror. We've been praying hard for God to take away the pain today, but I think now it's time I started praying for Christ to take us through the pain, to give us patience to see his miracle grow fully into grace. Then we can truly enjoy what he's prepared for us on the other side.

So what I'm saying is this: God is good. All the time. Please feel free to tell him so when you mention us in your prayers tonight.

Love you all!

Tuesday, September 22, 2015

Hello, loved ones,

Just wanted to let you know that Amy is resting comfortably this morning. She did have a little episode with nausea during the night but is doing better with that today. She's exhausted, partly as a side effect from all the medicines she's taking and partly just from the ordeal of yesterday, but at least we are doing a better job of pain management today. That helps her quite a bit.

We're still waiting for Christ to clear out the current bowel obstruction, so please continue to pray about that. I'd love to say we've seen lots of progress in this area, but I can't. I can tell you that we've seen hopeful signs for progress, so we're cautiously optimistic.

Also wanted to spotlight our pastor, Greg—you made me cry this morning, bro. What a joyful expression of support and love. For those of you who don't know, for all intents and purposes, Greg has declared this Sunday Mickey Mouse Day at our church (as a show of solidarity with Amy) and encouraged the entire congregation to come to worship wearing a Mickey adornment. So fun. We love you, Greg and Belinda!

Anyway, that's where we are today. We love you all!

Wednesday, September 23, 2015

Shh! It's been so long since this house has been quiet, I want to take a moment to hear the silence. Ahh.

Our girl is doing much better today. She's worn out but able to back off some of the pain and nausea medications that leave her feeling exhausted and loopy. And we're seeing the first bit of progress on overcoming the bowel obstruction—hallelujah!

Amy is still weak and still in some pain, but she slept nearly 24 hours and is improving today. It was a joy for me to see her fall asleep about ten minutes into an episode of *The Big Bang Theory* again. It's been a while since she had enough energy to laugh at her favorite geeks.

Anyway, thought you'd want to know we're having a peaceful moment right now and enjoying every bit of it. Thank you for your prayers and many kindnesses!

Thursday, September 24, 2015

Hi, loved ones,

So sorry—it's been a little hectic today, and I haven't been able to give you an update until just now. We got a little off on Amy's medicine schedule this morning and have spent the rest of the day trying to catch up.

First, the praise: Diarrhea abounds! (I know, you thought this was a family friendly group, didn't you?) We are grateful, as uncomfortable as that is, because it means the bowel blockage has been cleared. Of course, now Amy feels nauseated every time she has a bowel movement, and she's having several in a day, so it's kind of a two steps forward, one step back thing. Still, we are grateful because that blockage was causing her a lot of pain. (By the way—did you remember to thank God for your completely normal bowel function today?)

Amy is very weak still. (We went to the Cancer Center to have her bandages redone, and she nearly passed out in the waiting room.) And she really misses her work. She keeps talking about when she can go back, wishing she was at the conference in Chicago this week and wishing she had a manuscript to edit. She even misses the never-ending meetings that consumed many of her days. She had hoped to return to work by next week, but it looks like that's going to have to wait a while. This depresses her, but she's trying to keep the long view in sight.

Anyway, today was a little bit of a challenge, both physically and emotionally, but we avoided having to go back to the hospital—yay!—and she still has a few seasons of *The Big Bang Theory* left, so there is cause for joy in spite of it all.

Thanks for your continual patience and love and support. We love you all!

Tuesday, September 29, 2015

Today we go back to the doctor for the mid-chemo-treatment checkup and to find out what the long-term schedule is for the rest of Amy's chemotherapy series. Hopefully we can also find out how to better control her nausea and discover why she seems to be getting weaker day by day instead of stronger. Will let you know how it goes.

Later...

OK, here's how it went at the doctor's today...

No surprise, the doctor's biggest concern is Amy's weight loss. She now weighs 103 pounds and is very weak. The big difficulty appears to be that Amy has had such trouble eating solid food without sparking a bowel blockage—a consequence of the tumors left inside her abdomen. The doctor wants Amy to try easing into a "soft foods" diet to see if that can help reverse the weight-loss/weakness trend without aggravating the bowel again. So today Amy ate some mashed potatoes and a small portion of cottage cheese. We're hoping she'll be able to (1) not throw up everything she eats and (2) not have any bowel troubles after going off the liquid diet. Feel free to speak to Jesus about these things next time the two of you are chatting it up.

Amy's next chemotherapy treatment will be October 8. Although we will go back into the toxic / exhausted / weakened immune system cycle again, we are cautiously hopeful because our doctor thinks that after this treatment, we will begin to see a difference in Amy's bowel condition. Something more to pray about! Looks like the chemotherapy will run through the end of the year, with recovery into January. Amy would like to be done with it all by the time our second grandchild is born in February. Another thing to mention to Jesus for us.

As a side note, Amy is already lobbying the doctor to let her go back to work a few hours a day. Never mind the fact that (1) she can't get out of bed for more than an hour at a time without being exhausted, (2) she has had only one day in the past two weeks when she wasn't vomiting, (3) her bowel has been yo-yoing between blockage and diarrhea for weeks now, (4) she's still taking narcotic pain medicines to keep up with strenuous activities like eating, going to the bathroom, and watching *The Big Bang Theory*, (5) she is almost literally a 98-pound weakling, and (6) she still has cancer mucking up things inside her. Irrelevant details as far as our girl is concerned, I guess. Fortunately, our doctor was encouraging her about returning to work sooner rather than later, but he also gently suggested a little more patience before diving back into that world. So everybody at Group Publishing, you should know that Amy is missing you and can't wait to get back to your hallowed halls that surround Moose Butte Lane.

Looks like this is going to be a long journey, folks. Thanks for sticking around for so long. You are, each and every one of you, an answer to our frequent prayers. We love you!

2

Does Your Husband Love You?

Wait patiently for the LORD.
Be brave and courageous.
Yes, wait patiently for the LORD.

PSALM 27:14 NLT

Thursday, October 1, 2015

Well, the soft foods experiment is over. Back to a full liquid diet and bowel blockage protocols again. We'll try again in a few days. Thanks for your prayers!

Friday, October 2, 2015

Hi, prayer buddies,

Dr. Rubatt called us in for more tests to see if our girl needs IV nutrition. We'll see. I made Amy carsick on the 1.5-mile journey home, so my front yard got a little extra moisture when we got to the house. Then we verified that two of my bathrooms are in fine working order as we tried to get her back into bed. Guess I should take "old lady driving lessons" before taking my girl out on the road again. And, um, it's time to do laundry. Anyway, Amy's resting now...

Later...

I'm going to take the weekend off from posting, so I thought I'd give you the "here's where we are right now" summary, because even though I won't be posting, I'm still hoping you'll continue to pray. (I know—how selfish am I?)

The doctor decided not to do IV nutrition but gave some instructions for other things to try to help Amy recover a bit. She said she couldn't tell if Amy's current condition is a reaction to the chemotherapy or if the tumors were still wreaking havoc inside, and she preferred a conservative approach at this point. So we're doing everything we can to keep Amy as comfortable (and not vomiting) as possible.

Yes, there is another bowel blockage going on, so that just magnifies all the other problems.

Amy is safely out of the "nadir," when she was especially susceptible to outside infection. (Yay, we can hug her again!) I had thought people could come visit her this weekend, but it's hard to tell now because she's had such trouble with pain and vomiting. (Thanks, Jeanne, for not minding that Amy threw up during most of your visit today!) I guess we'll just play it by ear. If you are planning to come visit, check in first to see how she's doing.

Special thanks to our friends Kevin and Maureen for sending us season 8 of *The Big Bang Theory*. Amy likes to watch the show when she's exhausted or trying to distract herself from nausea and/or pain. Penny and the boys make us both laugh, which is good medicine. So, KevMo, you rock. Thanks.

Thanks also to the HR department at Group Publishing for the fun Soft Kitty blanket and slippers. It made Amy smile when she opened the box. A smile always looks good on her.

I do love that girl's smile.

Our conversations with Christ presently focus on the minute-by-minute stuff and go something like this: Let's knock out that bowel blockage, please. And wow, vomit is gross and unpleasant. Can we stop that recurring nastiness so Amy can keep food in her system, please? Also, as you know, Amy is weak and needs nutrition, strength, and weight gain. Hey, you created her body to need those things, so we're trusting you to provide them. And thanks for your constant presence and comfort. I'm amazed that anybody could go through this kind of experience without you nearby. (**P.S.** The people you've sent into our lives to accompany us on this marathon are pretty cool too. Nice job, Jesus.)

All right! Now you know everything I know. Thanks for your kindness, faithfulness, and undeserved generosity toward us. We love you all!

Saturday, October 3, 2015

Well, Amy is back in the hospital ER with severe dehydration and maybe some kind of electrolyte imbalance. She is saying some pretty interesting things. It would be funny if she weren't so vulnerable and innocent right now. Maybe we'll laugh about this later. Meanwhile, she could use your prayers. Thanks!

Later...

Quick update: Electrolytes are actually fine, though she's definitely dehydrated. On IV fluids right now. No explanation yet for her cognitive impairments—maybe a reaction to the nausea medicine? She is aware that she's having cognitive difficulties, and it frustrates and embarrasses her, but she's coping as best she can. They can't confirm a diagnosis as to why this is happening. They just took a CT scan on her brain as a precaution.

And yes, X-rays confirmed a bowel obstruction. They're talking about an NG tube[1] again, which Amy is NOT happy about. We're praying that this part of the equation solves itself before a tube becomes necessary.

Later...

CT scan is clear—no problems in the brain. Whew. The doctor thinks maybe it's a reaction to the nausea medicine. Amy is still a little confused but seems more coherent.

Meanwhile, back to the bowel blockage problem. They've admitted our girl to the hospital and are putting in an NG tube. Amy is not happy about this, but the doctor was insistent.

The doctor said Amy may need to have a second surgery to fix the bowel blockage thing, so the chemotherapy treatment scheduled for Thursday may not happen after all. Amy is not happy about this either.

Bonus—her hair is starting to come out in small handfuls, so everything is all kind of piling on at once. Amy is discouraged but trying to be a good patient.

---

1. A "nasogastric tube" is a tube that goes through the nose, past the throat, and into the stomach. No fun.

Bad day today, but we are still confident of better days ahead. *Soli Deo gloria.*[2]

Later...

Long night ahead. Amy is now unaware of her surroundings, and her mental fog is making her a danger to herself (since she has so many tubes and lines running in and out of her body). The hospital has stationed a nurse in the room for the night to act as sentry, and Amy's dad is there too. I've gone home to try to sleep in case tomorrow is anything like today.

They've tried a few things, but nothing has helped her so far. In fact, she's gotten worse. Mostly, she just needs to sleep, so let's make that the focus of our prayers tonight. God is always good, and he alone knows what's going on in Amy's brain tonight. I'm grateful he is constantly nearby to hear our cries and give us strength: "I know whom I have believed, and am convinced that he is able to guard what I have entrusted to him until that day" (2 Timothy 1:12).

Thank you for your prayers and love!

Sunday, October 4, 2015

Here's the latest. Amy is still in full delirium. She is unaware of her surroundings and pretty much dreaming and acting out her dreams. A nurse is in her room 24-7 to keep her from accidentally hurting herself (she keeps trying to pull out the NG tube because she thinks it's something else). She's a very active and strong-willed girl. Fortunately, her dreams all seem to be about family and about work (which she loves). Our granddaughter's name comes up frequently, as do the names of all our nieces. She has also, on several occasions, mistaken the nurse in our room for our son, Tony. You get the idea.

---

2. "Glory to God alone."

They've run a billion tests and still are uncertain what's causing the delirium. A tech is in here now attaching wires to her head to run an EEG, which she says will tell if there is any seizure activity in her brain. All of Amy's chemical levels are good (including potassium and electrolytes). The current theory is that maybe a bacterial infection, combined with her medicines and weakened physical state, sparked this condition. We are still waiting on the results of a blood test to confirm that diagnosis.

Two or three doctors are working on Amy now—our regular cancer doctor, an internist, and another doctor (I don't know what he does). Everyone is being very helpful and attentive, but we haven't made any progress.

Our cancer doctor gave us the difficult news that Amy's chemotherapy will have to be suspended for the time being, especially if there's a bacterial infection—it's too risky. But that just prolongs any recovery, which will be hard for Amy to take when she is back to her senses. We were all kind of pinning our hopes on the idea that the second chemo treatment would be the one that would help her turn a corner on the cancer. She had picked a target date to go back to work not long after the second treatment. She will be very disappointed.

In the answer-to-prayer department, Amy did have a bowel movement this morning. (Thank you, Jesus, for nurses who don't mind cleaning dirty linens!) So at least there is progress in that area. Meanwhile, we have another long day ahead.

And by the way, today is the twenty-ninth anniversary of the day Amy and I got married. So glad she said yes! There's no place I'd rather be today than where I am right now.

OK, now you know everything I know.

Ready…set…pray!

Later...

On the bright side, for about 30 seconds, Amy realized where she was and what was going on. On the downside, Amy realized where she was and what was going on.

She started weeping and told me, "I don't feel normal anymore. I just want to feel normal." Of course that just made the sit-in nurse and me start crying too. Now Amy is back in her dream world. Pray that she can feel normal again soon.

Monday, October 5, 2015

Hey, friends,

We are seeing signs of progress. Amy is coming out of the fog for short periods of lucidity. She remembered who I was this morning and has been able to wake up enough to carry on a few coherent conversations. Then she goes back to sleep and starts acting out her dreams again, but I will take any progress I can get, regardless of how short or how small.

Earlier this morning she told her sister Jody, "I know I'm living in two realities. In one, Bugs Bunny is walking around, and in the other, I'm in the hospital." Again, this is progress. Yesterday she was mostly unaware of even being in the hospital. Even though she continues acting out her dreams, she is much less agitated, so those of you who have been praying for peace, we are seeing God's Holy Spirit move in that area. Thank you.

I had a good conversation with our doctor this morning. They still don't know what is causing the delirium. All the tests they've run have come back negative, but our doctor still thinks it's a bacterial infection, and the fact that it seems like Amy is slowly responding to the antibiotic is one of the reasons why.

I asked the hard question today: If complications from this cancer are preventing us from treating the cancer, at what point does the cancer become untreatable? Dr. Rubatt was thoughtful and honest but also encouraging. She said the obvious. All these setbacks are taking a toll, and Amy's odds keep going down because of them. But she also said that at this point, she's not ready to say this fight is over. She promised not to keep us in the dark if things get to that point.

Meanwhile, we continue to have confidence that Amy (and all of us) are safely kept in Christ's care regardless of how this plays out. We do not see this circumstance as a reason to question God's goodness, but we see God's goodness as a reason to question our perceptions of this circumstance. We have known his grace and mercy too intimately for too many decades to do otherwise. As I said before, Christ is not simply a self-help philosophy or intellectual decision but the living, active Creator who inhabits every moment, pleasant or difficult, in our lives. I know him, he knows me, and the same goes for Amy. He is always enough.

As you pray today, mention to Jesus our gratefulness for his constant goodness. Also ask for continued progress for Amy—it's very nice to see our girl smile and know that it's for me again. We ask for mental clarity, true rest, peace, and strength. The first step in that is mental clarity.

Thanks for joining us on this long journey. It's an unusual friend who would walk this way with us for this long and not faint or give up by now. We love all you unusual people!

Later…

More later, but Amy has had a breakthrough, and I wanted to let you know right away. We are shedding many tears of love and joy. She wants you to know she loves you all.

Later...

All right, as promised, here's a little more detail on the events of tonight...

After Amy's sit-in nurse healing-massaged her legs this afternoon, our girl FINALLY fell into a deep, dreamless sleep for the first time in three days. The nurse and I tiptoed and whispered and pantomimed because we were so afraid of disturbing her! At one point we needed to readjust Amy's head because she was sleeping at an uncomfortable angle. It took us nearly a half hour before we could find the right moment and the right way to do it! But we did it, and Amy slept peacefully for nearly four hours. It was heaven. When she woke up (around 7:30 p.m., I think) she was kind of dazed at first. She asked what day it was. I told her it was Monday, and she said, "It's night already?" I said yes. Then she asked how long she had been out of it, and I told her since sometime during the night on Friday. She seemed really tired still but coherent and fully aware for the first time in days. She sat up on the bed for a few minutes, and then the new sit-in nurse helped her go to the bathroom and brush her teeth. Amy's father was also there with us.

She came back to the bed from the bathroom and sat down but didn't lie back down. She was so lost in thought, I worried that maybe she'd lapsed back into her dream world, but she was fine. She was feeling a deep heaviness, a great loss, over the fact that it was so easy for her to "lose time," as she called it— that she could just wake up and find that three days had passed without her knowing it. She said she remembered only snippets of the time, and most of it was people telling her not to pull the NG tube out of her nose.

OK, so now I have to interrupt and admit something that many of you know already. I'm a big crybaby. Even the hospital cleaning lady gave me a hug today because she felt sorry for my blubbering. Anyway...

I started sobbing because it was just such a relief to have my girl back. Of course, that got her crying too, and even her dad joined the crybaby party. Amy spoke of her love for us (and we of our love for her), and we talked frankly about the possible outcomes of this illness. She wanted us to know that if this cancer takes her, she wants us all to celebrate her life and not let her death be something that divides us or makes us bitter toward God or each other. She said several times, "I want my life to be something that brings people closer together and closer to Jesus." She said that time is so easy to lose, that we must treasure every moment we have together while we have it. She said she wants to stay, to live, because she feels like there are so many girls and young women she still needs to help—to build into their lives and help them grow closer to Jesus. But at the same time, she said that if that's not what God wants, then she's also ready to go.

I think that this kind of conversation (amid many tears, remember!) was uncomfortable for her dad. Maybe he was worried she was giving up on life, but she wasn't giving up or anything like that. It was just important for her to be able to talk about end-of-life issues and feel safe telling us what was important to her—what she wanted us to know and remember about her.

In the end, we all cried and hugged and laughed a little and cried some more. (For the record, I am NOT pretty when I cry, and I tend to cry at just about anything, so that means I am often unpretty. You'll have to get used to that if you plan to stick around.) Then she rested again but didn't go to sleep—just rested while we hovered around her, occasionally chatting with her. I finally left around 9:00 p.m. or so when the RN came in to check on her breakthrough and make sure she was comfortable. And I must have said "Thank you, Jesus" about a zillion times during the four-and-a-half-minute car ride home. So that's where we are tonight.

She's a special girl, our Amy. I think you all know that.

And she has great love for so many, including all of you. Maybe soon we can start having visitors come see her again. I'll gauge how she seems in the morning and let you know.

Meanwhile, I'm extremely grateful to Jesus for his kindness and attention these past three days…and deadly exhausted. I expect as soon as I shut off this computer that I'll sleep pretty hard myself tonight too.

We love you! Thank you for sticking with us in good times and bad.

Tuesday, October 6, 2015

Amy is resting peacefully. We are so grateful. She has made a point to talk to all her siblings today, just to tell them she loves them. She's so sweet and generous. (They've been showering their love on her too, by the way!)

Anyway, that leaves me sitting here in the room, feeling reflective. I have a good friend who told me once that he thought it was a mistake to say "I love you" to your spouse every day. He said it cheapened the sentiment, making it an everyday, unspecial thing. We had to agree to disagree on that one, because for decades it's been my habit to tell Amy I love her before she gets out of bed in the morning and again before we go to sleep at night (and anytime in between that I feel like it, which is, you know, a dozen times or so a day). It is an everyday, ordinary thing between us, I'll admit, but never unspecial. I found out how important that silly little habit was this past weekend.

There was a time on our twenty-ninth anniversary day when Amy couldn't remember who I was or what her last name was. To try to help her remember her last name, I asked her, "Are you married?"

"Yes," she said.

"What's your husband's name?"

"Mike Nappa," she said.

"Does he love you?" I asked.

Instantly she said, "Yes. Very much."

I wonder what her answer would have been if I'd followed my friend's idea of not saying "I love you" every day. I'm glad I don't ever have to find out.

And by the way…I love you all!

Wednesday, October 7, 2015

Well, we finally cut off all of Amy's hair. It was falling out in chunks, so she asked her mom to come do the deed. (Thanks, Winnie!) She says she looks like a cancer patient now, but she is in good spirits about it all anyway.

She mentions frequently how glad she is to be free of that dreaded NG tube.

She's been on the IV nutrition since 6:00 last night, and we can see a difference. Amazing what a little protein can do for the body. The plan is to keep her on this to make the next chemotherapy session possible. They are fine-tuning the nutrition mix to best fit her physical needs, hoping to make her good and strong for dealing with the harshness of chemotherapy. Based on the improvement this morning, we are cautiously optimistic. She's clearheaded and relaxed—still fighting pain issues, but the doctors and nurses are helping her cope. She keeps telling us all that she loves us, which, as you may have guessed, we haven't gotten tired of yet.

We're praying for a restful day, more strength, reduced nausea, and consistent pain management. We're so grateful to have a little boredom in our day so far. We've had enough adventure for the time being.

We love you all!

Thursday, October 8, 2015

(From Amy!)

Hello, dear friends!

I am able to post a greeting myself today! I have been on IV nutrition for more than 24 hours now and am feeling significantly better! We are still working on the right pain medicine and are doing better with pain management too. The current plan is for me to go home on Friday with the IV on a home plan. Please pray that all the logistics with insurance and the home health agency get worked out for that.

For the next few weeks, I will only "eat" clear liquids, such as broth and some juices. The nutrition from the IV will be enough.

I cannot thank you all enough for your precious prayers. You all are a treasure for me, and I am beyond grateful for you!

Keep me in your prayers!

Friday, October 9, 2015

Hi, loved ones,

So this is kind of an odd request. We are looking for a family who is willing to adopt probably the sweetest longhair Chihuahua in the world. After what we've just been through with bacterial infections, it's just too risky to keep an animal in the house. Plus, poor little Swarley is living in neglect recently, as my attentions have been distracted elsewhere. Anyway, here are the details...

Swarley is an AKC registered purebred longhair Chihuahua. He is seven years old (he'll be eight November 27). He is well socialized, and children adore him. He loves to sit on your lap while you watch TV, so he totally earns the name "lap dog." He has been trained not to bark (ask anyone who has come to the house, and they can testify to this), so he's definitely NOT the yippy, annoying kind of dog. He's a soft bundle of fluff, weighing in at a whopping five pounds. He's house trained, but he's never been around other dogs, so if you are thinking of adding him to a group of dogs, you might want to consider that. He loves to play with his Mickey Mouse plush toy, to sit in the sun, and to cuddle.

If you have kids in your house, you will make them very happy when you bring Swarley home.

If you are retired or just someone who hangs around the house a lot, you will find great joy in this little dog. We are sad to see him go but are happy that he will be going to a new, safe, loving home.

Let me know if you are interested in giving your family happiness and love for the next seven or eight years.

We love you!

Friday, October 9, 2015

(From Amy!)

I'm home!

Saturday, October 10, 2015

Today Amy was tired of being cooped in her bedroom at the world-famous Nappaland Suites, so she's sitting at the dining room table, sipping on tasteless broth, and catching up on some mail.

I'm in the living room, trying (unsuccessfully) to take a power nap in a comfy red chair. Suddenly I hear choked sobs coming from the kitchen. "What is it?" I say, worried. "Are you OK?"

"Yes," she says and sniffs miserably. "I'm just reading these cards and am so humbled by how my friends keep loving me."

She points to one card and says a name. "This person has sent me a new card every week." She points and says another name. "This is the second card I've gotten from this person, and I don't even know her really. She's a friend of Annette's." She holds up two cards. "These are from the same person—she sent me two cards on the same day." And there's still a small stack of cards left unread on the table!

OK, you know me. Now I've joined in the waterworks (but we'll leave that part out when we tell it to the press).

And so our girl had a good cry because she's so overwhelmed by the fact that you love her, that you haven't forgotten her, that despite your busy lives, you seem to be sticking with her for the long haul.

Don't you folks know it's been two months already? Can't you see how draining and slow this fight against cancer is going to be? Aren't you aware that you're going to get frazzled and worn out and that you're supposed to forget about Amy while you soldier on through your own lives? It's almost Christmas season, for goodness sake! How will you ever keep up?

No mind, I guess. Maybe you will fade before the finish line. It doesn't matter. Today Amy felt your love deeply, and so today, in spite of everything, was a very good day. Thank you. We can never adequately express our thanks for you, so now we're just thanking Jesus and asking him to give you a raise at work, the best parking space at the grocery store, and the finest chocolate on sale at half price.

We love you!

P.S. It has been my responsibility to keep track of all the gifts and kindnesses you have given us so that we can be sure to eventually send you an appropriate thank-you card. Sadly, I'm bad at my job. In fact, the past ten days I've forgotten completely to fill out my ledger, and now there's stuff everywhere. I haven't the slightest idea who sent it or brought it over. I'm so sorry! We are so thankful for your many kindnesses, and the reason you'll never get a card telling you so is my strange kind of brain freeze. Please accept my apologies, and for what it's worth,

THANK YOU!

Sunday, October 11, 2015

I'm so grateful to report that Swarley has found a new, loving family that has welcomed him in with open arms…um…paws. We adore his new owners and are certain Swarles is already glad to be there. Thank you!

Monday, October 12, 2015

(From Amy!)

Well, friends—it is official. I am bald. I had a few patches of hair left that looked pretty odd, so yesterday Mike buzzed those spots off. Annette told me I'm still beautiful, and I am believing her! My head had been chilly for several days, so I had already been wearing a hat—now I'm even sleeping with one!

Thanks to those of you who have given me hats. I am putting them to good use.

So far the nighttime, at-home IV of nutrition is going well. I am getting used to the sound of the machine and the fact that I have to get up often to use the bathroom. It is pumping a lot of fluids into me over 12 hours each night. Mike and I have both learned how to do all the hookups to the IV.

Thank you all for continuing to pray. I do see small improvements each day. That's encouraging! Love to you all!

Tuesday, October 13, 2015

(From Amy!)

Here is my good news for today. I have been cleared to work up to ten hours a week from home. Today I spoke on the phone with some of my coworker friends who I have not talked to for almost two months. Great feeling to connect!

Prayer request: I have chemo on Thursday. I have missed some previous chemo treatments due to health setbacks and really need to get back on schedule. Please pray that I stay healthy these next days so I can complete this important part of my treatment. Thank you so much! I love you!

Thursday, October 15, 2015

(From Amy!)

Hello, friends and family. I am at chemo! Have been here all day and still have an hour to go. I had a lot of pain and throwing up yesterday, and this morning was still a bit rough, but once I got plugged in and started treatment, I have felt much better. Thanks so much for all the encouraging words and prayer. You have no idea how much you all mean to me!

Saturday, October 17, 2015

So here's something I never thought I'd brag about: Amy didn't throw up all day long! Woo-hoo! Thank you, Jesus!

That's my first update after chemotherapy treatment #2. My second update is to say THANKS to everyone for your faithfulness toward us these past weeks. It was a serious answer to your prayers and ours that she even made it to treatment #2. We are grateful that Christ has given an opportunity for Amy to at least put up a fight against this disease. And we're grateful to you for praying us through this time. The first thing she did at chemotherapy on Thursday was run to the bathroom and throw up. Then she slid into the chair and tried to rest while the compassionate nurses hooked her up and started her on pre-chemo stuff. After some nausea medicine and a dose of morphine, she felt better. By the end of the day, she'd made it through the full chemotherapy session, and she came home comfortable and alert.

Today Amy is still weak (weighing in at 99 pounds this morning) but definitely seeing benefits from IV nutrition. She hasn't been able to eat much more than clear liquids for almost two months now yet doesn't complain. In fact, she spends a lot of time experimenting with broth mixtures ("How about strained onion soup with beef broth today?") and apologizing for "being a bother." Whatever, right?

She's also struggling with a prolonged, accelerated heart rate that sometimes adds to her exhaustion. Doctors haven't yet been able to explain the rabbit race going on inside her chest, so they're keeping an eye on it. At this point they're hoping that problem will correct itself.

Amy keeps a sense of humor in spite of everything, and by the way, she absolutely LOVED being able to reconnect with her coworkers for ten hours this week. She will be one of those people who, on her deathbed, says, "I wish I'd spent more time at the office."

Tomorrow is day four of the second treatment cycle, and if it's like the first cycle, we expect extreme fatigue for a few days. After that comes the dreaded "nadir" period from days 7 to 14. During this time in the first cycle, Amy contracted the bacterial infection that wreaked havoc, sent us back to the hospital, and prompted us to give away our beloved Chihuahua. Needless to say, we're stocking up on antibacterial wipes and approaching the upcoming nadir with a little apprehension. You know what to do about that, right? (Hint: It involves calluses on your knees...)

For now, though, we're going to let tomorrow worry about itself and just enjoy the moments we have together today. She's a special girl, as you all know. She and I are pleasantly surprised to find that there are plenty of good times during this generally awful season. Her smile is breathtaking, and thankfully she gives it away often and for free, even during her pain. (Hey, Mom, I married a good one, huh?)

Keep our girl in your prayers, please. It's hard to see her suffering so much and for so long. Please ask Jesus to give her strength, to work his healing through the chemotherapy drugs, to reduce the strain on her beautiful heart, and to protect her from any new complications or infections. Thank you! We love you!

Monday, October 19, 2015

Sometimes writing a book is like writing a letter to yourself. Today I flipped through a forgotten book I wrote a few years ago and read these words about Jesus calming the storm: "When that whirlwind inevitably happens, I've learned that you and I have two choices: (1) We can surrender *to* our circumstances, or (2) we can surrender *within* our circumstances. We can let our circumstances define the way we live our lives...Or within any circumstance we can look to Jesus, trusting him for help and guidance and letting him determine the outcome."[3] That made sense to me then, and it continues to make sense to me now. It's a good reminder from my past self that what I know is true on sunny days remains true on stormy ones as well.

Today was uneventful here at Nappaland (yay!). It was a welcome space in a stormy season. Amy is still losing weight (she registered at 98 pounds today) and is a little discouraged to find out that her IV nutrition has to be adjusted to 14 hours instead of 12 because of a warning sign in her blood work. But on the other hand, today was the first day in about two months that our girl went an entire day without needing pain medicine just to cope. We are hopeful this is a sign God is using the second chemotherapy treatment to make progress against the cancer inside her.

We also got some mixed blessings from our insurance. The first envelope I opened was documentation that our insurance company had paid more than $37,000 in hospital bills for Amy (whew!). The second envelope was a notice of denial of service from the insurance. Our doctor wants to attack the cancer with both IV chemotherapy and an oral chemotherapy drug that targets something specific that showed up in Amy's genetic testing results. The oral chemo would make it hard for the cancer to return after it goes into remission, but our insurance has denied coverage of that treatment. Hard news to hear, but we know that Amy's future doesn't lie in the hands of insurance companies or even in various medical treatments. Christ alone holds Amy's life in his hands, and so we choose to surrender within this circumstance as we wait to see how he intends for this to shake itself out. Besides, you needed something new to pray about, right?

As always, we thank you for your continued prayers and for your many kindnesses (including the two wonderful women who scrubbed and sanitized

---

3. Mike Nappa, *God in Slow Motion* (Loveland, CO: Nappaland Communications, 2013), 71.

all our bathrooms today in preparation for the upcoming nadir in Amy's treatment cycle!). And we are grateful for the blessing of a mostly uneventful day. Keep praying for strength, for Jesus to work his healing through the chemotherapy drugs, for the strain on Amy's heart to subside, and for God to protect our girl from any new complications or infections. We love you!

Tuesday, October 20, 2015

First, today we are thankful for (1) no pain medicine needed two days in a row! Big, big deal here at Nappaland. *Gracias a Dios!* (2) A whole week's worth of IV nutrition bags delivered right on time today—yay! (3) *The Big Bang Theory* season 8. It just makes us smile, which makes us grateful.

Here are a few things to remember in prayer: (1) Amy is still losing weight. Today she was down to 96 pounds. Friends, that's not a lot of Amy left. At this point she's lost 20 percent of her body weight in just two months. This is a serious concern. You know what to do. (2) Amy still isn't able to eat anything but clear liquids (which doesn't help the whole weight issue). Today we experimented with a single serving of cream soup. If her bowel doesn't block up, we'll try again tomorrow as well. Hoping we can slowly reintroduce real food into her system without getting back on that whole bowel-blockage, run-to-the-hospital freight train again. (3) Some of our IV nutrition equipment has been faulty the past few days. We've been able to work around it and get timely help, but it's starting to make us feel stressed. It'd be nice if everything just worked the way it was supposed to work instead of making it exciting for us every time we go to hook up the nutrition bag. (4) Nadir starts Thursday. Needless to say, we're a little nervous this time around. We've seen firsthand what bacteria can do.

We're so glad you continue to stand beside us through this. Just so you know, we can never repay you for all your kindnesses toward us…but we're going to keep receiving your blessings on us anyway. (No backsies!) We love you!

Wednesday, October 21, 2015

(From Amy!)

Hello, everyone!

Just a short note to say today has gone well. Thankful each new day to see what God has in store and ending each day with praise for even small graces. I am still off pain meds and am taking a lot of precautions because now is the time where I am extra susceptible to infection. Trusting God and so, so, so thankful for each of you who is praying. Much love to you all!

Thursday, October 22, 2015

(From Amy!)

Hello, friends!

Many of you have asked how you can help. Well, here is a need that I'm hoping a few of my local girlfriends would be willing to do. It's a little odd though!

You may not know that my parents have been sleeping in the bedroom across the hall from me almost every night of this journey. My dad spent every night in the hospital on a cot, and Mom has taken shifts too. Because of Mike's own health issues, he is not able to help me if I call in the night for medicine or help (which I rarely do…but it does happen), so they have slept across the hall in case I need anything.

My parents leave soon to go back to Arizona for the winter, and we are wondering if there are any girlfriends who might want to sign up for a regular night to stay over. You would need to arrive around 8:00 p.m. and stay until around 7:00 a.m. You could shower here if you want and leave directly for work or go home—whatever works for you.

Think about it whether you might be able to sign up for a night on a regular basis. If you are interested or want more info, you can message or text me and we can talk! Thanks!

Sunday, October 25, 2015

(From Amy!)

While we are not able to go to church, we blast worship songs through the house and sing. Half the songs make us cry—God is so faithful and worthy of praise!

Monday, October 26, 2015

It's been nice to see Amy feeling well enough to post for herself on Facebook lately—thank you, Jesus! Still, I thought you all might want a longer update on life in Nappaland this week…

1. Amy has now been out of the hospital for the longest amount of time since she went in for surgery in August. Yay!

2. Our girl weighed in at 99 pounds today, so weight is still a significant concern.

3. Amy hasn't needed any pain medicine since her last chemotherapy. This, we've decided, is due to both the chemotherapy working and God's healing hand accelerating the work of the chemotherapy drugs. We are so grateful.

4. Amy still can't eat food and is still is on a clear-liquid diet, though we're beginning to experiment with cream soups in the mix once or twice a day. She's taken to smelling my food just to remember what it was like to eat with a fork and from a plate. We hope to be able to transition to a "full liquid" diet after the next chemotherapy session. We just have to be very careful not to do

anything that could cause another bowel obstruction, which would send us back into the hospital and postpone chemotherapy treatment again.

5. IV nutrition has been a godsend. Sure, we'd love for Amy to be able to eat food, but lacking that ability at present, we are so grateful that she can still get what her body needs directly through her PICC line. She has much more energy and alertness, and (bonus!) this kind of "designer nutrition" (formulated specifically for her unique body) helps her build up the strength needed to handle the chemotherapy treatment.

6. We are in the middle of her nadir period for this round of treatment. This time we are being scrupulously rude about protecting our girl from random bacteria and germs. Sorry! We're just treating you all like family. Amy's sister Jill is coming to town to help out this week, and since we know that airports are a haven for all kinds of exotic germ mixtures, we're making poor Jilly shower and change clothes before she can even see Amy. Same thing for her brother, who is visiting later in November. In fact, I shower and change clothes after I do something as simple as grocery shopping. We learned the hard way what a little bacteria can do, and we have no desire to risk having to endure that kind of trial again.

7. Amy's next chemotherapy session is November 5, and the one after that is scheduled for Thanksgiving Day (though it may get moved to the day before or the day after). We are cautiously optimistic, as the November 5 infusion will mean she's halfway through the full treatment plan. Our goal is simple: Get. Amy. To. The. Next. Chemotherapy. Session! God willing, she'll be done with this series of treatments by the end of January 2016.

8. Amy's birthday is coming up—November 10. Because of her near-quarantine and just the way things are right now, we don't really have anything planned for that day, or for Thanksgiving or Christmas. This is OK with us—actually, it's a little bit of a stress relief because it means we don't have to worry about adding extra holiday tasks onto our quarantine and chemotherapy. Still, we may invite you all to a "Winter Holidays in Spring!"

party come next March or April. So don't pack away those Christmas carols after the New Year—just in case.

9. Amy has been LOVING getting to work a few hours each day and has been so encouraged by all of you at Group Publishing, so thanks for helping make her job easier. She's already making plans for when she's allowed to work more and has made herself a little workstation in her bedroom with a telephone, computer, and stacks of manuscripts and other odds and ends. She misses her work the most, I think, which is funny because she used to say I was the workaholic in the family. Now we know the truth.

10. I'm up to number ten already? Clearly I talk too much.

I think that's enough for now. Please continue to speak to Jesus about us. Be sure to let him know we're grateful for his constant presence with us and kindness toward us, for the healing signs we are seeing in Amy's body each day, for the little joys that sprinkle the moments in our day (and that usually make us cry). And please ask for continued progress for healing, for complete removal of pain and nausea, for strength and weight gain, and...please get us to the next chemotherapy treatment without any setbacks! Thank you all. We love you!

Wednesday, October 28, 2015

(From Amy!)

Today I am looking forward to a short walk outside with Mike (hold on, sunshine—wait awhile, clouds!) and seeing my sweet sister Jill, who is coming out from Arizona for a week. Reasons for joy!

Thursday, October 29, 2015

All right, we saw our oncologist today. Turns out that two months ago she sent a biopsy of Amy's big tumor to a large cancer research lab in Phoenix for specialized, detailed analysis. They identify special DNA markers in tumors and then, based on current research and other incomprehensible stuff, create a curated list of chemotherapy drugs that are most likely to successfully treat individualized cancer markers. It's kind of a designer-recipe approach for cancer treatment options, individualized for a single patient's unique circumstances and cancer pathology. It took two months to get the results, but they finally came last week, and our doctor showed us the full report today.

Amy is currently on two chemotherapy medications, and of the two, one of them is listed in the report as having a very good success rate against Amy's personal DNA cancer markers. Yay! The second one, though, is listed as having a low probability of success, so our doctor says it's not worth the side-effect risks of that second one to continue it. She is discontinuing that second chemotherapy medication.

In its place she wants to use a third chemotherapy medicine (no, I don't remember the name) that will attack a specific marker that showed up in this report but didn't show up in earlier pathology reports. Apparently this third medication has a strong history of success against Amy's specific kind of cancer marker. Our doctor seems very optimistic about this change in the treatment plan.

The one big risk in making the change is that this medication causes one out of eight patients to experience some level of cardiomyopathy (irregular heartbeat and possible heart attack). That's a little sobering, especially since Amy's heart rate is already higher than is healthy or normal. Because of that new risk, they are going to monitor Amy's heart carefully from this point on, including a heart scan/test today to get a baseline. Additionally, the chemotherapy series will take a month or so longer for Amy to complete, which is not ideal. At any rate, the new chemotherapy regimen is scheduled to begin on Thursday, November 5.

Obviously, we're excited to discover how they can pinpoint Amy's DNA markers and prescribe chemotherapy treatments specific to them, but we're also concerned about that whole "Hey, this might give you a heart attack" kind of thing too. Still, we're trusting God's care and attention, and we're expecting him to guide Amy and her doctors through this whole process in the way he knows is best. He is always good, regardless of the circumstance.

All right, by now your knees should be in veteran fightin' shape, so you know what to do. We love you!

Sunday, November 1, 2015

(From Amy!)

Psalm 16 has been my favorite for years, and during this cancer journey, it still holds true. (Go read it!) Our dear friend Eric Jaqua wrote a song for me as a gift—the lyrics are directly from Psalm 16. I get choked up every time I listen to it. God is right beside me in this. He's right beside you too! Happy Sunday, my friends!

Tuesday, November 3, 2015

My family (hi, Mom) has kindly pointed out to me that I've missed a few days of updates—so sorry! It's not that things are not happening; it's just that sometimes I can't keep up with everything that's going on, and well, sometimes I just choose sleep instead of posting. Sorry! But I will correct that failing right now.

It has been an adventuresome few days here in Nappaland, though mostly good days. And this post is long, so feel free to skim to the end if you don't need all the minuscule details of our mundane life…

1. We continue to be humbled by the selfless generosity of our friends and family. There have been too many kindnesses to even mention them all, but two moments stand out today. Our first "Amysitter" showed up right on time tonight, cheerful and not grumpy at all about having to sleep in a borrowed bed—well, on a thin mattress spread out hastily on a couch in a tiny bedroom—all so she can be nearby just in case Amy needs a little help during the night. She's so generous, and there are many more of these wonderful Amysitters coming—so many that we'll have an Amysitter in the house every single night of November. Wow. It's so humbling to even need that and even more humbling that so many of you are willing to give that time and kindness so freely to us. You rock. Also, yesterday I used up the last King Soopers[4] gift card that people so generously gave a month or two ago. I said a prayer of thanks for that at the time. Then today one of you gave us ANOTHER King Soopers gift card, just because! What a blessing. You folks are too cool.

2. Amy is (mostly) doing well, within the circumstances. Our single focus each day is simply to do everything we can to make sure she doesn't miss her next chemotherapy treatment. So far, so good! She had one day when her bowels struggled, which gave us a little scare, but by the next morning God had worked everything out in there, and we are back on track. Yay!

3. We continue to be militant about germs. Sorry to everyone who is Amysitting or who stops by to say hi! If you've been in an airport, we are making you shower and change clothes before you can see Amy. When I go out to run errands or go grocery shopping, I come home and shower and change clothes before I see her. We wash or Purell our hands frequently (I had to start adding lotion to the regimen because I made my hands bleed, which is also unsafe for Amy). Sick people have to stay away (even our beloved granddaughter, sniff). We are being very careful about touching and about

---

4. Our friendly neighborhood grocery store.

"sneezing distance," which are the two main ways germs are transferred (air and skin). I'm sure I've offended many people by being unwilling to shake their hands (sorry!), but, you know, I hated shaking hands before Amy got sick, so at least now I have a good excuse. Thankfully our efforts seem to be paying off, as Amy has avoided any new infections over the past few weeks.

4. Amy is still not able to eat any solid food. She eats mostly clear liquids but has tried introducing two bowls of cream soup a day. She had one day when that cream soup seemed to slow things down, so she added water to it to make it less thick, and that seems to have solved the problem. We are hopeful that after the next chemotherapy session she will be able to begin introducing more "full liquid" foods like cream soups and dairy. We'll have to wait and see. Meanwhile, the prescription for her IV nutrition runs for about one more month, so we're hoping she'll be ready to eat real food before then. (Something to pray about.)

5. Speaking of IV nutrition, they tinkered with the formula last week, and it seems to have helped. She is still skin and bones (103 pounds today), but she is slowly adding a little weight, which is an answer to prayer. Thank you, Jesus!

6. We have some kind of doctor's appointment every day this week, which is both stressful and helpful. It's just a lot to keep up with, but we are grateful to find excellent medical care just a mile or so from our home. Yet another blessing from God.

7. The next chemotherapy treatment is on Thursday. I don't know the name of the new drug they are trying this time. The old one they are keeping is carboplatin. We'll see how Amy does handling the new drug and its side effects and let you know how it goes.

8. Some people have expressed a desire for a group to come by the house on Amy's birthday next week. It's so sweet of you—but just for safety and convenience, I'm going to ask for no "drop-bys." It's certainly sweet of you to want to help Amy celebrate, but it causes difficulties on our end. Maybe you'd consider sending a video instead? Or scheduling individual visits? Thank you!

9. Amy is in good spirits, taking joy in little things, like being able to walk around the block (twice!), and in big things, like being able to work 15 hours a week from home. (She gets so energized when it's time for her to work—like a child ready for dessert!) We continue to find many grace moments in each day. It's kinda cool. Plus, Amy is fun to hang out with when she's not vomiting her guts out or nearly passed out from pain. So that's nice.

All right! Now you know everything I know. We're grateful for your prayers. When you and Jesus are hugging it out this week, mention Amy to him, asking for protection for Amy from any new infection, strength to handle chemotherapy, progress in weight gain and the ability to eat, total avoidance of any new bowel blockage, and mitigated side effects from the new chemotherapy drug. Whew! Good thing you've had some practice at praying. Remember, it only takes 10,000 hours to become an expert at something, so hopefully Amy is helping you become an expert on your knees.

I'll let you know how things go after Amy's next chemotherapy session on Thursday. We love you!

Wednesday, November 4, 2015

Saw the doctor today, and Amy was declared fit enough to handle the rigors of a new chemotherapy session. Yay! That means two things:

1. We are so grateful that Amy has avoided any new infections and has grown strong enough to receive the next chemotherapy treatment. It's an answer to prayer. Thank you for praying us through to this point!

2. Thursday, November 5 (Amy's chemotherapy day) is hereby declared "International Mickey Mouse Apparel and Creative Display Day." Every time you see Mickey, remember to say a prayer for our girl as she's getting poison pumped directly into her bloodstream. We have to kill off that cancer if we want to see her get better.

You know what to do!

Thursday, November 5, 2015

For those of you who are bored and curious, here's what our life has looked like recently in random moments of a day…

Yesterday we went to see the doctor to make sure Amy would be cleared for today's chemotherapy session. Our normal oncologist is out of town this week, so we saw our doctor's partner for the first time. Going into this one, we knew two things about him: (1) He's an accomplished hematologist/oncologist with a stellar reputation around northern Colorado and (2) he always seems to be running behind schedule on his appointments. (We found out why after we met him—the guy is a real talker! Told us all about his daughter, his gay friends who moved from Boston to San Francisco, his fondness for San Diego, his recent family trip to Disneyland, and so on.)

Anyway, Amy and I are waiting in the exam room, and the doctor is late, and there's a whiteboard with markers on the wall. We are nothing if not self-entertaining, so first I tried to draw a Mickey Mouse symbol on the whiteboard. Unfortunately, my artistic skill is about as good my talent for imitating vocal accents (more on that later), so pretty soon I erased sort-of-Mickey and drew a hangman game instead. What followed next was a spirited, nail-biting contest between Amy and me. We chose movie titles as the theme, and back and forth we went. I thought I had her on the ropes with *Big Top Pee-wee*, but she got it at the last possible moment. Dang! Then she stumped me with a movie she loves and knows I hate: *The Godfather*. I was just making my big comeback with *Minority Report* when the doctor finally came in, a good half hour late. (For the record, I did at least stump the doctor with *Minority Report*.) That meant I lost the game, but still, I'm glad I married a girl who's a good date when you're sitting around waiting for a tardy oncologist to tell you it's OK to pump poison into your wife's body to fight a cancer that's nearly killed her.

A few days ago, Amy and I were just hanging around the house talking, and I was thinking about the big picture of this whole cancer thing. Amy's cancer is genetic, meaning she inherited it as a part of her DNA, which also means that her sisters and brother are at risk for developing similar kinds of cancer.

"So here's a question," I say to her. "Knowing what you know now, knowing how awful this experience has been…if God had come to you six months ago and said, 'Someone in your family has to have cancer in order to prevent the others from getting it,' what would—"

And before I can even finish the question, Amy interrupts me. "I would have volunteered," she says immediately. "I don't want anyone I love to have to go through this. I'd rather it be me than anyone else."

Funny thing is, her suffering may have accomplished just that kind of thing. By going through this cancer fight, she has exposed the danger of hidden cancer to her younger siblings and even our son. So now all of them are having genetic testing done to see if they inherited Amy's kind of cancer DNA (there's a 50/50 chance they have). If that test comes back positive for even one of them, that family member will have time to take action to prevent duplicating Amy's experience. It's almost as if God said to himself, "I need a volunteer to endure cancer so others can avoid it. If I asked Amy, I know what she would say…"

Last night we got a new thriller novel in the mail. Amy and I were sitting around in her room, killing time before the Amysitter arrived, so I started reading it aloud to her. (Side note: When I read a book aloud, I always make lame attempts to "do the voices" so the characters don't all sound the same.) As I'm reading aloud this scary thriller that starts with violence and suspense and possible creepy things going on, I notice that the character narrating the story is using words like "flatmate" and "hoovering around" and other British lingo. Ah, I say to myself, this character is British, so I start reading in what I think is a passable, if not perfect, British accent. (After all, Amy expects me to "do the voices," right?) But instead of hushed silence and edge-of-your-seat suspense on Amy's bed, I hear sudden snickers and giggles. I look up, and she finally stops holding it back. Full-on laughter that squinches her eyes shut and shakes her whole body is flowing out of her.

"What?" I ask. "The character is British, so I'm doing a British accent!"

Amy laughs even harder. "No you're not," she gasps at me. "You're *trying* to do a British accent, but..." And we're back to the laughter.

At first I'm all wounded and disappointed. (Come on, old chap, is my Brit accent *that* bad?) But then I realize how wonderful it is to hear her laugh—just that transparent, open laugh that makes you feel like you're listening to music and want to sing along. So what could I do? I joined in. And then, after we'd both settled down, I went back to reading it straight American style. Ah well, nothing is perfect in life, now is it? (But don't tell Amy: I'm secretly practicing my British accent anyway. I think it may come in handy next time I read *Harry Potter* aloud to her!)

We love you all!

Monday, November 9, 2015

Amy is a little beat up from the new chemotherapy drug, but she's holding up well, all things considered. For her birthday, we are going to try introducing frozen yogurt into her diet. Feel free to pray that it all goes down (and out) well! Thank you!

Later...

OK, so here's the official story: "Gosh, Mike Nappa is so sweet. Did you see that he shaved (most of?) his head in support of his poor cancer-stricken wife?"

Got that memorized? Good.

Now here's what really happened: Amy has cut my hair ever since we were engaged, meaning I haven't paid for a haircut in 29 years. *Why start now?* I think to myself. *That's like, 12 whole bucks better spent on comics.* So my girl tells me this week it's time to get a haircut. "Sure," I say, "no problem." And tonight, after she goes to bed, I pull out the electric clippers.

How hard can it be? I think. *See, it's easy as...oops. Well, I can fix th—wait a minute. Dang. All right, how about if I...uh-oh. Better start thinking of an "official story" for the current state of my head...*

I'd post a picture for you all, but I'm worried you might choke on your breakfast from laughing too hard, and well, I don't want to be responsible for any mirth-related injuries. Suffice it to say, Amy has an interesting birthday surprise waiting for her when she wakes up in the morning.

But remember, if anybody asks you, your response will be, "Gosh, Mike Nappa is so sweet. Did you see that he shaved (most of?) his head in support of his poor cancer-stricken wife?"

Got it? I knew I could count on you.

Oh, and adding insult to idiocy, I cut my ear shaving afterward. (Yes, my ear. Long story.)

Life is rarely boring over here in Nappaland.

Love you all!

Tuesday, November 10, 2015

(From Amy!)

Thank you to everyone for the wonderful birthday wishes and for continuing to pray. Having cancer on my birthday was not my favorite thing, but there is no doubt I have felt loved and encouraged today. I have cried many times just because I can't express how much I feel cared for. Thank you all so much! (Yes. I'm crying even now.)

Sunday, November 15, 2015

I can't sleep because you all have been on my mind and in my prayers for the past few hours. Nearing the end of this conversation, I finally realized, "Hey, maybe God is reminding me that people would like to have an Amy update today." (Yeah, I'm frequently that oblivious to the obvious, so it's a good thing Jesus is patient with me.)

Anyway...

1. **Physically, our girl is holding her own lately, a genuine relief.** The combination of chemotherapy and IV nutrition has strengthened her body some and helped her stabilize physically. When I say "stabilize," I don't mean "back to normal"—that's just not realistic at this point. It will still be months before Amy's life looks anything like normal. But at least she's no longer in serious physical danger. She's still very much underweight, but they've been adding calories to her IV nutrition, so she's managed to weigh more than 100 pounds (yay!). And she hasn't needed pain medicine for weeks now—a true blessing. She still is not able to eat anything but the simplest of foods, though, which is difficult. Her prescription for the IV nutrition runs out the first week in December, so we need to get her back to eating soon. It's just a slow, hard process, and progress is measured in inches instead of yards. Feel free to make this a matter of renewed prayer if you think of it.

2. Emotionally, Amy remains as strong as ever. She's tougher than her 100-plus pounds would suggest. She's learning that it's OK to be sad about having cancer and that there is joy to be found even in the most depressing of sorrows. (How weird is God to do something beautiful and strange like that? He's so cool.) Her birthday was probably the hardest day for her. Normally that day would be chock-full of family and laughter and delicious foods spread all over the house, and I think she mourned the loss of that just a little bit. Plus, I forgot to do my Liz Lemon dance for her, so that had to be disappointing. (Sorry, hon!) She's still prone to sudden tears and fits of gratitude every time she reads a new batch of encouraging cards from you or witnesses again her friends giving so generously in myriad ways (cleaning toilets, making airport trips, buying groceries for us—you name it). If it's a blessing of any size or shape, you people have done it for us. How weird are you to keep doing things so beautiful and strange and loving like that? (You're so cool.) We find ourselves being grateful quite often, which, given the circumstances, would seem unusual if we didn't know you.

3. Our girl has put her foot down with me as well. As some of you know (hi, Vicki!), I'm supposed to be writing a novel right now. My publisher has been very patient and supportive through this whole situation, so that's good. But Amy wants to read my next novel—which I haven't written yet. In fact, I haven't worked at all for the past three months (for obvious reasons), and Amy is determined that I get back to the task at hand. I told her I'll start writing again when the time is right and tried to leave it at that. Ha. She was, um, unsatisfied with that response. She said I need to stop constantly worrying over her and write her a new book instead. Then she pulled out the big guns. In case you don't know this, my wife controls me through prayer. Whenever we reach an impasse, she simply says, "I'll start praying for God to change your heart." I hate it when she says that. It means that if I'm in the wrong, Jesus is going to bring it up with me in ways I can't avoid. Long story short, it looks like I'll be keeping office hours next week. The rule is I have to work as many hours a week as her doctor allows her to work, which right now is 15 hours a week. (Yes, if her body would let her, she'd put in many more hours than that. She's itching for the day when she can work 50 hours a week again…but I digress.) Anyway, it takes me a LONG time to write a novel, and 15 hours a week isn't going to cut it in the long run, but it's a start. And I'm terrified that I've forgotten what to do or how to tell a new story or, most likely, that I'm really just a fraud faking my way through a writing career. (For hard evidence of this, see the abysmal sales of my last book, *God in Slow Motion*. 'Nuff said.) Anyway, if you happen to think of me during your prayers, I'd appreciate it if you'd mention this whole "Amy wants a new book and won't take no for an answer" problem to Jesus. Let him know my wife will be mad at me if he doesn't help me do a good job on this one. Thanks.

4. We had a little good news this week. We had thought switching to the new chemotherapy drug would mean that Amy's treatment would have to continue into April of next year, but we found out that the plan (at least for now) is for Amy to finish chemotherapy in February. Yay! There is, of course, a recovery period after the last chemotherapy infusion, so we're not sure what that means in terms of the overall schedule, and we could possibly get to the end of this treatment plan only to discover more treatments are needed. But for the moment, we can see a final act on the horizon in this little tragicomedy. This is encouraging because up to this point, Amy's condition has been so open-ended, with so many unexpected setbacks, that it was hard to see where or when the applause might appear. But now we have an end date to look toward, so we're thanking God for that.

OK, this post is plenty long now—time to wrap up.

To summarize, you are way cool. We are way grateful for you. And God is way good. He is always good.

We love you!

Tuesday, November 17, 2015

(From Amy!)

One week of trying soft foods and still doing well. Today added in a smoothie. Tomorrow get to have guacamole (no chips—just the guacamole). So far all is moving through with no blockage.

And even though it was pretty chilly today, I was still able to go for a short walk. Mike is not a fan of walking, but he's my hero. He faithfully goes along with me each day the weather permits.

Thankful for these blessings! And thankful for each of you! We are blessed to have so many dear friends faithfully praying for us.

Thursday, November 19, 2015

Today we invented the Hugging Shirt (patent pending). Yep, it's pretty much exactly what it sounds like.

We took one of my snap-up long-sleeve shirts (Mickey apparel, of course) and dedicated it to Amy's room "For Hugging Only." When Amy wants to love on someone, or when she just needs a little lovin' herself, she'll put on the shirt over her clothes and wrap the sleeves around one lucky person for as long as is necessary. When they're done, she'll take off the overshirt and hand it to me. I will disinfect the shirt (either with Lysol spray or Clorox wipes— so no, it's not like it's the sweetest-smelling shirt in the world, but at least I won't have to wash and dry it after every use) and then return it to its rightful place next to Amy's bed, where it'll be ready to serve when the next huggable moment arrives.

We tested out the Hugging Shirt (patent pending) tonight with Amy's sister Jody. Except for all the teary slobber and gross mucous that dripped onto the shirt during the hug, it seemed to hold up just fine. I mean, we're not ready to mass-produce or anything just yet, but for the moment at least our girl can get a little sweet comfort when she needs human contact—without exposing herself too much to bacteria living on other people's clothes. So we're counting today as a win. (Thanks for beta testing the shirt, Jody!)

Anyway, that was our big deal for today. Not exactly rocket science, I know, but it did cheer us up a bit, and I figured you'd want to know about it. And by the way, thank you for all your faithful prayers and encouragement! Amy takes great comfort in your presence with her during this time. God is constantly good to us, and you are evidence of that every day.

P.S. Wouldn't it be cool if every family had a Hugging Shirt hanging in the living room? Then whenever you had a bad day or just felt a little lonely, you wouldn't have to say anything—you could just put on the shirt and signal your family members that you're hungry for a huggin'. Hmm. Maybe you should try that this week and let me know how it goes.

P.P.S. Obviously, your Hugging Shirt should be some kind of Mickey apparel. Duh.

P.P.P.S. Um, when you're wearing your Hugging Shirt, would you also let it be a reminder to say a prayer for Amy? (You know, "prayer hugs" instead of "air hugs." That kind of thing.) Thanks!

P.P.P.P.S. We love you! Duh.

Later...

(From Amy!)

Some of you have commented that I am brave and strong in this cancer battle. I try—but I also want to be honest that it is dang hard. Last night I had a weepy meltdown. This road is so long, and I am tired of it. I want to pick up my granddaughter and play with her. I want to hug my family and friends. I want to go to church, work, the gym. All of that is still months away for me. And poor Mike has to listen to me when I get like this. I thank God that Mike is so patient with me. So today will you pray that I have renewed courage and strength and resolve? Thanks!

Saturday, November 21, 2015

Here's the weekend update…

1. We're now entering our second night of a broken furnace at our house. Apparently there's some lame danger because our gas meter regulator is broken. That, in turn, is causing our furnace to leak gas and carbon monoxide before it turns on each time. Whatevs. We're kicking cancer's butt over here—ya think we're scared of a little odorless, colorless, deadly gas? But our heating service guy insisted, so now we've got several space heaters decorating the hallways while we wait for Monday to come so we can ask the gas company to replace our meter regulator.

2. On the bright side, I'm saving a ton of money on shampoo. Ahem. ("Gosh, Mike Nappa is so sweet. Did you see that he shaved most of his head in support of his poor cancer-stricken wife?")

3. Amy is holding her own. The Hugging Shirt is getting plenty of use (love you, Brianna and Alexa Brolsma!). And she ate ramen noodles yesterday without incident. Who'd have thought that ramen noodles could both (a) get us through college and (b) be used in treating cancer? Also, she so appreciated all your encouragement when she was struggling emotionally earlier this week. You guys rock. (Except that we kept crying every time someone shared a new Scripture or generous word with us. Oh well, so we're crybabies. I think you guys knew that already.)

4. Amy's prescription for IV nutrition runs out December 7 (four days after

her next chemotherapy treatment), so that's our target date for getting her to be able to eat on her own.** The good news is that the IV nutrition is doing a good job of giving her strength to tackle each new chemotherapy session. The bad news is that we have to figure out how to match what the IV nutrition is doing for her but on a limited "soft foods" diet. We'll figure it out, but feel free to pray about that transition. We don't want her to go back to being a 96-pound weakling who can barely get out of bed.

5. We're also trying to wean Amy off the nausea medicine. Pray that it goes well! (So far, so good…)

6. Little blessing alert: Our oncologist is going to be out of town during Amy's next chemotherapy. Something about finally taking a honeymoon in Hawaii. Like Hawaii with your new spouse is more fun than staying in frigid Colorado in December so you can see Amy and me for ten minutes on a chemotherapy day. Some people just have warped priorities, I guess.

Anyway, last Thursday our oncologist was walking by the Cancer Center while we were there to get the dressing changed on Amy's PICC line. She saw us and stopped just to check in with Amy. She sat in the windowsill next to Amy for a good 20 minutes, asking about all the things doctors ask about, giving us advice (Hugging Shirt, anyone?), and approving work time for Amy. Oh, and she told us about that silly Hawaiian honeymoon thing, like that was important. Anyway, it was just a little blessing for us to get to see her spontaneously like that and very kind of her to sit and talk with us until all our questions were answered. (OK, so now I hope she has a good time in Hawaii, even though I'm pretty sure Amy's cancer could be treated in Hawaii too, but well, we weren't invited. As my niece taught me, "Whatevs.")

7. (Do you think I use parentheses too much?)

I think that's enough for now. When you're hanging out with Jesus in the coming days, be sure to thank him for his kindness toward Amy, and let him know we're a little stressed about the upcoming transition from IV nutrition to soft foods nutrition but also excited for the progress. As always, we're just grateful he stays close by with every new step in this adventure.

Love you all!

Sunday, November 22, 2015

OK, sorry for the delay in posting. I was watching football and trying not to think about all the crazy things happening in our house.

Anyway, here's the story behind yesterday's post about our furnace. On Friday we had our heating guy come out for the annual winter tune-up on the furnace. Usually that takes about 30 minutes, a new filter, and he's done. After he'd been here for about four hours, I finally asked what was going on. He said our furnace was leaking gas and carbon monoxide and he was trying to isolate why. He finally said that the problem was with the regulator on the gas meter outside and that we needed to have the gas company replace it so the gas pressure would level out inside the furnace.

Today I woke up and thought it was Monday, so I called the gas company. Turns out that when a gas leak is involved, they work Sundays, so a repair guy from the gas company came out today. He looked at the gas meter and said, "Nuh-uh, tell your heating guy there's nothing wrong with that." Then he said, "Well, tell you what, your gas meter is really old, so I'll go ahead and replace the meter and the regulator both, but tell your heating guy he's wrong and it works just fine."

Afterward, he said that since he'd had to turn off the gas line while working, the pilot light in our water heater had shut off. He offered to relight the pilot. When he opened up the water heater, he stopped, took out some fangled mechanical instrument, and took a measurement. He said the water heater was leaking gas, that it was a hazard, and that he was obliged by law to condemn it and shut it off until it was replaced with a new water heater.

I said, "So let me get this straight. My furnace *and* my water heater, which both worked just fine on Thursday, are suddenly *both* independently leaking natural gas—and yet there's nothing wrong with the gas company equipment? It all just spontaneously happened here inside my house?" (OK, so maybe I was a little sarcastic. Sorry, gas guy, I know you were just doing your job.)

The guy just shrugged, shut off my water heater, slapped a big red "Hazard" sign on it, told me to call my heating guy, and left.

What could I do? I spent the rest of the day watching football with my brother-in-law. Isn't that what you're supposed to do when this kind of thing happens?

Anyway, despite this little adventure, God is not surprised, nor is he helpless, and that means neither are we. We have a few days of inconvenience ahead of us but remain well cared for in a comfortable house full of space heaters that only occasionally overload and trip the circuit breakers and knock power out of sections of our home. We have access to showers just a few houses away at Amy's sister's house. And we have great companions (each other!) inside this house, people who enjoy being together regardless of which appliances happen to be working on any given day. And we have new stories to tell you—so, you know, we've got that going for us.

And honestly, we'd rather be here at home with no heat and no hot water and occasional blackouts than back in the sugared comforts of the hospital any day. So obviously, there's much to be thankful for. God is always good.

When you're praying tonight, feel free to chat with God about this new little glitch in our lives. We're asking Christ to help us get our house back in working order as quickly as possible—and at an affordable cost. (Good thing I've been saving my shampoo money!) Thank you!

Monday, November 23, 2015

(From Amy!)

Good news on the water heater! We can wait until I am done with chemo to replace it—it will have to be replaced, but not today. So we can at least plan for that instead of having to get it done immediately! Yay! Thanks for prayers. Still waiting for the heat to be done, but we still have space heaters, so all is well.

Later...

(From Amy!)

The heat is back on! Thanking the Lord!

Tuesday, November 24, 2015

Dang. Almost made it an entire day without crying. Then Candace showed up with a cake box, and the next thing you know, Amy and I are both little crybabies. Overwhelmed. If you work at Group Publishing, you know why. You all are kinder than you ought to be, and now I have a headache from crying, but we are very grateful for each of you. Remind me someday to tell you a behind-the-scenes story about this whole experience.

Wednesday, November 25, 2015

(From Amy!)

As Mike says, we were overwhelmed with the generous gifts from our friends at Group, who had a bake sale yesterday and blessed us beyond belief. I started crying again this morning just thinking about it! I am amazed at how

God continues to provide for us and how kind beyond belief our friends and family are. God is good. God is good. God is good!

We love you!

Friday, November 27, 2015

One five-year-old fake Christmas tree: about $80

Two boxes of ornaments collected over 29 years: $100–$200

Sitting on a couch seeing tree lights reflected in my girl's tears as she whispers, "I love Christmas. I'm so glad I'm here for it this year": priceless.

Tuesday, December 1, 2015

Believe it or not, the arrival of December means we're finally at about the halfway point in Amy's cancer treatment. Dr. Rubatt is targeting March 1 as the finish line, so God willing, we have three months to go!

Meanwhile, this month also signals some significant changes, so I'm hoping you've kept your kneepads in game shape. (I use a gardener's pad next to my bed—you could try that too if you don't have kneepads!) Here's what's happening…

1. Amy's next chemotherapy infusion is this Friday. Counting this treatment, she has three more total to go. Last time, we added doxorubicin (affectionately referred to as the "Red Death") to the chemo cocktail, which is supposed to better target Amy's specific brand of cancer. We hope it is doing that. We do know that adding the Red Death took a bigger toll on Amy last time physically—just left her feeling kind of beaten up for several days. We are praying for this next treatment to be effective and for Amy to be able to physically handle the aftermath well.

2. We are targeting December 7 as the day Amy finally goes off the IV nutrition! This is both good news and sobering news. The IV nutrition literally saved Amy's life, and its weekly formula, tailored specifically to Amy's body, has built up her strength and health and given her body the capability to endure chemotherapy. But it is artificial nutrition and can't be counted on as a long-term solution, so it's time to wean off that. This means we must find a way to replace orally all the nutrition the IV bag is providing. This is going to be a challenge because Amy still is unable to eat anything more than soft foods and liquids. We're meeting with a dietitian on Friday to help us figure out the plan. We're asking for God's guidance and grace as we make this transition—and for NO SETBACKS! We've had enough of those, we think.

3. From time to time, I've complained about frustrations with our insurance company, so I think I should also give credit where credit is due. Yesterday Kaiser saved us $500 in cash—and they didn't have to do that. We didn't even know about it, and they didn't have to tell us either. They just did it on our behalf without our asking. A blessing from God, yes, but also a gift from the insurance company (in addition to the many thousands they've paid in hospital and other medical bills). So for the record, I apologize for whining about insurance. I think sometimes I'm just a little myopic. (OK, most times…)

4. For the next three months, our primary goal will continue to be to get Amy to the next chemotherapy session. Everything we do each day will have that goal as a guiding factor.

5. Not related to anything above, but a little Christmas advice I discovered yesterday: If you're already the crybaby type (no names, please) and "O Holy Night" comes on the car radio, it's not a good idea to crank up the volume and try to sing along. Getting all choked up and weepy while driving on icy Loveland streets isn't the safest way to get home. I'm just sayin'.

All right, now you're all caught up on the "Amy Adventure." We're asking for you to get your knees back into praying shape, if you're willing. When you and Jesus are spending time together, please bring our names into the conversation. Ask Christ to continue to give Amy strength and health, for a smooth transition from IV nutrition to food, for NO SETBACKS!, and for effective, tolerable chemotherapy…and did we mention NO SETBACKS!? Also tell Jesus we are so thankful for his constant presence, frequent kindnesses, and the loving, encouraging, strong-willed, determined, patient people he's put in our lives. (Yeah, I'm talkin' 'bout you there!)

Ready…set…pray!

Friday, December 4, 2015

It's funny how things that once terrified you can later fill you with excitement and anticipation. Chemotherapy has been this for us.

When we first started this adventure, we were dreading chemotherapy. Hey, we'd heard the (horror) stories. And to be honest, some of them are true. But now we can barely wait until the next chemotherapy appointment, stamping our feet impatiently, butterflies flitting in our stomachs until the next infusion occurs. There are hardships from pumping poison into Amy's body once a month, but we are seeing the blessings of that poison as well. It's a vivid example of the truth that sometimes God will hurt you in order to heal you.

Amy has not needed pain medicine for nearly two months now. Whenever we tell our doctors that, they are always surprised. (I keep thinking, well, we do have a LOT of people praying about that, but I don't want to insufferably brag to the medical staff.)

Amy still needs nausea medicine but is only taking half doses at this point. We are cautiously optimistic that she might be able to kick that habit before the next chemotherapy infusion (December 31).

Amy's next big step is breaking free from the lifesaving IV nutrition. We are meeting with a dietitian tomorrow to help us formulate a plan for that, but that's the step that makes me nervous. We've come so far. It would be hard to bear another bowel blockage appearing, so please make this a matter of conversation next time you're on your knees.

We also got a new prayer request today—Amy's white blood cell counts are down and struggling to recover to normal levels despite all the extra shots and treatments they are doing to build those up. At this point, they are telling us not to worry too much about it (right, do they not know me yet?) and that they will keep an eye on it. Low white counts make Amy much more susceptible to bacteria and germs, and if the count drops too low, that could interfere with her chemotherapy schedule. So we will continue our over-the-top germ-prevention precautions (sorry!) and make this a regular part of our prayers from today forward. Feel free to do the same.

Chemotherapy went well today. Amy felt good, tolerated the medicines well, and even got to eat a little lunch at the Cancer Center (mashed potatoes and gravy and berry yogurt). And because we had plenty of time on our hands, I started reading a new book out loud to Amy to pass the hours. (It's a Newbery children's book I remember loving when I was 10. I'm still loving it 40 years later. And no, there are no British accents in this one.)[5]

Starting today, they are going to begin doing monthly blood tests to check for the presence of cancer inside Amy. There's some specific test they can run that reveals the marker for Amy's cancer. (The normal cancer-free level for that marker is 30. Back in August, Amy's level for that marker was more than 3,000.) We are hopeful this marker will be significantly reduced by the time we finish the chemotherapy series. Hey, that's something else you can pray about.

We continue to be overwhelmed and humbled by your loving care, kindness, generosity, and prayers now these many months down the road.

We love you!

---

5. In case you're wondering, the book is *My Side of the Mountain* by Jean Craighead George.

3

You Look Terrible

I know the LORD is always with me.
I will not be shaken, for he is right beside me.

PSALM 16:8 NLT

Friday, December 4, 2015

Well, here's a little curveball. I've come down with a fever tonight and have had to quarantine myself in the basement to protect Amy. It just feels like the worst time possible for this, as I am Amy's primary caregiver, and the days right after chemotherapy are higher maintenance. Plus we have the added stress of breaking free from the IV nutrition on Monday. Sigh.

Still, Jesus is not surprised by strange setbacks like this, and he even provided our friend Jennifer Hanes to Amysit tonight before we even knew that anything was wrong with me or that we would even need her. In fact, we'd planned for Jennifer not to be here tonight, but Amy changed her mind about that just because she missed seeing her. God is constantly at work in ways I never see or anticipate, preparing for blessings even amid discouragement. Thank you, Jesus, for Jennifer!

Anyway, please pray that whatever is messing with me right now will pass through quickly so I can return to my rightful place beside Amy.

Thank you!

Sunday, December 6, 2015

Well, we are now at the part of the cycle where chemotherapy is kind of beating up on Amy. She is very fatigued and subdued, which is normal but still no fun. She also has some abdominal pain and digestive discomfort. And she no longer has any appetite, which is probably OK for today because of the IV nutrition. But starting tomorrow, she goes off the IV and must eat nutrition whether she wants to or not. Pray that she will recover enough to want to eat. And for pain relief. And for no nausea. Thank you.

No news yet on the cancer marker test. We'll let you know what we hear when we hear it.

I'm still (mostly) quarantined to the basement because of an intermittent fever, which is really frustrating. I don't know why I keep having a fever, and I just don't want to risk exposing Amy to anything strange and new. I used gloves and a mask tonight to get her hooked up to the IV. Otherwise she's been mostly on her own up there. She doesn't complain, but I know it's harder on her. (She's such a social girl.) I can't get an appointment to see a doctor until Thursday afternoon. Hopefully I'll be all healed up by then and it'll all be a past-tense story.

Finally, for the record, if anybody asks, your answer should be, "Of course Mike meant to dye those brand-new white pillowcases pink. Why else would he wash white linens with a brand-new red blanket?"

You might want to memorize that.

We love you!

Tuesday, December 8, 2015

(From Amy!)

Hi, everyone. I have a new urgent prayer request. As you know, Mike has not been feeling well for a few days. He was able to see his doctor this afternoon, and they immediately sent him to the ER. It sounds like he is going to have to have surgery. It may be his appendix or it may be something else. They are getting ready to do a scan, and then we will know more. I will post details when I have them—but for now, please pray. I am contacting some of you to come and check in on me and to stay with me while Mike is in the hospital—and Mike will likely need some people to go over and check in on him too! Thank you so much for your care and love for us!

Later...

(From Amy!)

Latest update. Mike is being admitted to McKee tonight, and they are still deciding whether to do surgery or another procedure. The best I understand it is he has an abscess in or on his small intestine. They may need to do surgery to remove it. Or it might be possible to drain this with a needle—but there are risks with that option as well. The doctors will have to decide what is best, but for tonight he is in the hospital. I am doing OK—I have had people here this afternoon, and once again Jennifer Hanes is spending the night with me. I have people coming to check on me tomorrow and to spend tomorrow night, but I will need more people to come by and make sure I'm fine over the next few days. Mike is having a hard time not being here with me, but he is getting the care he needs. God is in control!

Later...

(From Amy!)

Last post for tonight. Mike is meeting with the surgeon in the morning. He will likely be in the hospital for five days—that's what they are saying right now. Please pray for comfort for him, as he is there alone. I hate that I cannot be there with him—this is very hard for me! Thank you all for listening and praying! Love to you all!

Wednesday, December 9, 2015

(From Amy!)

I just talked to the chaplain from the hospital, and she said Mike will have surgery this afternoon between 1:00 and 1:30. Right now Mike is very uncomfortable and is throwing up, so pray for him not to be so miserable as he waits for the surgery prep to begin. More updates to come…

Later…

(From Amy!)

I don't have any updates from the hospital yet, but one bright spot in my day is that my dad is coming out tomorrow to help. Thanking God for awesome parents who will fly out on a moment's notice. Dad will take great care of us, and I'm thankful that Mom is willing to let him be gone—it's a gift from both of them! I'll update again as soon as I know more about Mike.

Later…

(From Amy!)

Mike is in surgery. Praying for wisdom for the doctors and for the best possible result for Mike—the least pain and easiest recovery!

Later…

(From Amy!)

I finally have an update! Mike is out of surgery and is breathing on his own. He will be in recovery for a while, so no visitors tonight. The doctor had to remove about a foot of his small intestine and then sewed that together where she took it out. She said the bad news is she believes he has Crohn's disease, which his gastroenterologist (GNT) will have to treat. Mike will be in the hospital anywhere from three to ten days, depending on how long it takes him to…ready for this…pass gas and poop. So pray for a good recovery—and that he will be able to come home as soon as God is ready for him to be here.

Thanks for your prayers today—please keep them going, as Mike is going to need them for a while now! Love to you all!

Thursday, December 10, 2015

(From Amy!)

Our friends Jim and Robin went to see Mike this morning. They report that he is in pain from surgery but is looking better than before surgery. He says he can tell a difference in how he is feeling now compared to how he felt before surgery. I'm guessing today will be a lot of resting to recover from the surgery.

Today is Mike's birthday. Guess we will be celebrating sometime in the future! Thanks to you all for continuing to pray for my dear husband. I love him so much!

Friday, December 11, 2015

(From Amy!)

The nurses have had Mike up and moving about, trying to get his bowels moving. He is trying to keep his spirits up but is really struggling with pain from the surgery. As he faces the long night ahead in his room, please lift him up in your prayers. Mike says he knows Jesus is near, and he believes God is good. It's still hard to suffer and hard for me to know he is suffering. Thank you all for continuing to keep us in your prayers.

On my end, my dad is here and is taking great care of me. I am grateful that he could come and that my mom was willing to send him! I just wish Mike was at home and feeling great.

Sunday, December 13, 2015

(From Amy!)

As you can imagine, Mike and I are missing each other greatly. My dad had a wonderful idea today. He drove me over to the hospital, went inside, and had Mike come to the window in his room. He's on the second floor, but I could see him really well. We talked to each other on our phones while seeing each other through the window. We both were crying—it was so great to see him.

Mike is feeling very discouraged because he still cannot eat and is getting weaker. He is having trouble walking much but needs to walk to get his bowels moving. He needs to pass gas or poop but has not done either. It has been five days since he has been able to eat. That is part of why he is so weak.

Please pray that his bowels will wake up and start functioning again and that Mike will not feel so discouraged. We had hoped he could come home on Monday, but it is not looking like that will happen. The longer he is there, the harder it is for him.

I know you all are prayer warriors and you know what to do. As Mike would say, "Ready…set…pray!"

Later…

(From Amy!)

Huge answer to prayer! Mike has had "success" (you all know what I mean), and he gets to come home on Monday! WOW! I am so thrilled! Keep praying for recovery—but THANK YOU for prayers that are bringing him home to me!

Tuesday, December 15, 2015

(From Amy!)

The snow is falling fast here in Loveland, and it looks peaceful from my warm perch inside our home. My heart feels peaceful too, as Mike came home yesterday afternoon. We are all under one roof, and I am grateful.

Dad went to get Mike yesterday and spent the rest of the day picking up prescriptions, groceries, and other items. We are thankful we don't have to go anywhere today, as the snow is deep. Dad tried to get out to go to McDonald's to get coffee, but at the end of the driveway he decided to skip coffee today because the road was too snowy.

Mike is taking quite a few medications for the next week to manage pain, prevent infection, and so on. I know he is glad to be in his own bed though. It will be a few days before he's up and about. Thank you all for your prayers, which have gotten us this far. God continues to show his love for us through the actions of our friends who have prayed like crazy, brought food, cleaned our home, and on and on. You all are so dear to us, and we are humbled to have friends like you.

Sunday, December 20, 2015

(From Amy!)

Hello, dear friends! Mike is doing better day by day. He is weaning himself off the pain medication and is trying to eat foods high in protein. He is down 30 pounds according to the doctor. They confirmed that he has Crohn's disease, and he has an appointment next week with a specialist. We understand that he will start having infusions that will become a regular part of life from now on.

My dad is still here and will leave on Christmas day. He has been an amazing blessing—driving us to appointments, doing all the shopping and errands, fixing stuff around the house, and most of all bringing encouragement to us each day when we are feeling a bit discouraged by all of this.

Mike says he misses everyone. He promises to post after Christmas—he just needs a few more days to feel like himself again.

Today I woke up feeling worried and struggling to trust God with so much going on. But during the day, many joys have come my way, and I am moved to tears knowing that God has not forgotten me, and neither have my friends. Thank you all for continuing to pray for us. The journey is long, and we have needed you to hold us up so many times. We could not do this without you!

Wednesday, December 23, 2015

Hello, loved ones,

Please accept my apologies. I've been very delinquent about updating you. I can offer no excuses except to quote the immortal Greg Brady: "Something suddenly came up." One day soon, when I have some energy, I'll try to give you the full story. Meantime...

Amy ate one entire slice of cheese pizza yesterday!

If you've been following this group for long, you know why that simple sentence brings tears to my eyes. We find ourselves filled with exhausted gratefulness over silly things like that. It is a good time for life to make itself known, and we find such joy that life has come and is being celebrated wherever we turn. These days have certainly brought challenges, and yet today, two days before Christmas, we find ourselves warm, well fed, well cared for, well loved. And thanks to the irrational generosity of some of you, there are even a number of colorfully wrapped presents snuggled cheerfully under our Christmas tree.

And did I mention AMY ATE AN ENTIRE SLICE OF CHEESE PIZZA YESTERDAY?

Joy to the world, the Lord is come. In our house at least, it seems like he's here to stay.

We love you!

Friday, December 25, 2015

All right, this is l-o-n-g, so feel free to ignore it, or skim it, or whatever. But some of you have wanted to know exactly what happened to me this month— why I suddenly disappeared for a while—so here it is. Keep in mind that most of these memories were made while I was either in intense pain or under the influence of random drugs, so if I mistake dates, times, or conversations, well, that's just the way the memory has fixed itself inside my head. Sorry.

Early in November, some of my chronic abdominal pain and nausea seemed to flare up.[1] I figured it was just stress and tried to move on. By December we all knew I wasn't 100 percent, but I'd also had bouts of worse trouble over the years, and chronic pain and nausea have been a part of my life for nearly two decades, so I didn't think much of it. We stayed focused on the primary goal: Get Amy to the next chemotherapy! Our plan was working, sort of.

In early December, our friend Jennifer came over to Amysit for a night. As we were settling in, she said to me, "You look terrible. Take your temperature." I kind of felt terrible, so I did and was very surprised to find I was running a fever near 102 degrees. This was soooo frustrating because it meant I had some kind of infection and had to quarantine myself from Amy. Grrr. That night I sweated it all out and was back to normal the next morning. Whew. Until nighttime came around. Amy insisted I take my temperature. By bedtime

---

1. You know, that chronic gastritis stuff I mentioned earlier.

it was back up over 101. This cycle repeated itself until Amy finally convinced me to call a doctor.

I've been seeing a GNT for many years, and I always go to him first for anything related to my stomach or digestive system. I called and spoke to his nurse. She said I could see my doctor in February. I gently suggested maybe he could work me in sooner than two months from now. She not-so-gently suggested that I either go to my family practice doctor or to the hospital. I opted for neither—until my girl gave me a lecture. So I finally made an appointment with my family practice doctor. The earliest I could get in to see her was a week away, on December 10, my birthday. So I went back to my quarantine and waited.

On December 8, my GNT called. His nurse had told him I called. He asked what was up. I explained I was having abdominal pain, had lost a lot of weight, and had some crazy intermittent fever that I couldn't seem to beat. "I need to see you today," he said.

"Your nurse said you weren't available," I said.

"We'll call you back in a minute," he said. A minute later his nurse called and said I had an appointment in one hour to see my GNT. "Good," Amy said. "You can get an antibiotic prescription, and then we can be in the same room again." Sounded reasonable to me.

My friend Jimmy cleared his calendar and generously drove me to the doctor. (I guess if I didn't feel safe to drive, that should have been a clue to me that maybe I was sick, but I never claimed to be the smartest guy in the room.) An hour later, Jimmy and I are sitting in the exam room at my GNT's office. The doctor walks in and stops.

"You look terrible," he says. (Why do people keep saying that to me? It's not a compliment, you know.) Then before he even examines me he says, "You have to go to the emergency room."

I try not to roll my eyes. "I can't do that," I explain. "My wife is going through a difficult chemotherapy treatment regimen right now."

"Get up on the exam table," he says. Then the, um, male heir of a female dog (love you, Mandi Nappa!) taps a spot on my belly that makes me feel like screaming. "You have to go to the hospital," he says again. "Right now." (Stupid Jimmy, who is supposed to be my friend and supposed to take my side in all things, has now jumped out of his chair and started gathering my things.)

"Look," I say calmly, "can we just put that off for two more months, just long enough for Amy to finish her chemotherapy?"

My GNT is unsympathetic. He starts talking to Jimmy about getting me to the hospital. There are vague suggestions of surgery, but now I'm not listening. These people seem to be taking matters into their own hands, regardless of what I say or want.

"Can't I just get that antibiotic prescription?"

My GNT is suddenly in my face again. "I'll call Amy," he says to my nose. "I'll talk to her personally and tell her what's going on. But you need to go to the hospital."

Jimmy answers for me: "Yes, we'll go right now."

Fine. Whatever. I stop at the desk on the way out. "I need to make my copay," I say helpfully to the lady. "I think it's $40." She starts to pull out the paperwork, but Jimmy steps between us.

"He's not making a copay today," he says. "He's going to the emergency room."

I have my wallet out, credit card in hand, but the lady closes her books. "OK," she says to Jimmy, and he pulls me out the door. I'm beginning to wonder if maybe he just did a cool Jedi mind trick or if maybe I'm turning invisible or something. The *Star Wars* theme song plays alongside "Mister Cellophane" somewhere in my subconscious. Later my wife will tell me that my GNT did call her—right then. He told her I was "wild with concern" for her and instructed her not to let me come home. I think that was a bit of an exaggeration. Yes, I was concerned about Amy, but it's not like I was foaming at the mouth or howling at the moon or something. Doctors. Drama queens, all of 'em.

Next thing I know, December 8 is almost gone, I'm hooked up to an IV in a room on the second floor of the hospital, still not sure why the ER doctor insisted on admitting me for an overnight stay. A strange German woman I've never met breezes into my room and cheerily tells me she's my surgeon.

Wait. What?

She happily explains that a CT scan has shown I have some kind of awfulness in my small intestines. (We later learn that it is "a pathology consistent with Crohn's disease" and that I've apparently had it eating away inside me for quite some time.) She pauses to blow her nose on a soggy shred of tissue. Tomorrow, she continues, real gusto in her voice now, she's going to slice through my belly button and rip out my insides with her bare hands. Something like that. And I can't decide if I'm more traumatized by the fact that I'm about to undergo an emergency operation against my will or by the apparent reality that my surgeon has a raging cold.

Then, just before she breezes out of the room, she stops and asks about my drug allergies. "I'm allergic to pretty much all narcotic pain medicines," I tell her. She frowns. "Then how am I supposed to treat your pain after the surgery?"

Um…no one told me there'd be a test.

There's an awkward silence while we both stare at each other, waiting for the other to say something. I break down first. "I honestly don't know," I answer. More silence. I think I've flunked a pop quiz and maybe she's disappointed in me.

Then she forces a smile. "Oh well, we'll figure out something." Not exactly a big confidence booster, strange lady who is going to split my stomach open like a melon, but I try not to show any concern. I'm beginning to feel like I'm in a really bad improv acting class, and for some reason I'm supposed to say, "Yes, and…" every time she says something that makes me want to pee in my tattered blue underwear. I opt for saying nothing as she whistles into the hallway with bloodlust on her mind.

And then the world kind of blends together into a dark smudge of time passing. (Yeah, I think I was in shock for a while.)

And it's suddenly the next afternoon, December 9, and I'm waking up, and I can't breathe because I'm writhing in so much agony, and I'm wondering why I have to wake up anyway because when you're in great pain, aren't you supposed to pass out to escape for a bit? But this guy, Nurse Tim, keeps waking me up anyway. (Yeah, OK, they told me later they had to keep waking me up because I stopped breathing whenever I passed out. Twice they did this to me. Just for a silly thing like breathing.) At any rate, I finally figured out I wasn't going to be allowed to pass out, so I just started screaming for help instead. Hey, it made sense at the time. As I recall, my screams sounded something like this: "Help me, Jesus! Help me, Tim! Help me, Jesus! Help me, Tim!"

Finally, after about six or seven months and two road trips to Alaska, Nurse Tim gets off his lazy butt and says he's going to help me, but I have to stop thrashing around. (Whatever. You try not thrashing around when they won't let you stop breathing.) "I'm going to give you three Tylenol suppositories," Nurse Tim says, and I'm thinking, *I don't care what you shove up my, um, posterior, Timmy Boy. Just do something to make me stop screaming.*

Aloud, of course, all I say is, "Help me, Tim! Help me, Jesus!"

And then the deed is done, and I'm suddenly very thankful that Nurse Tim knows his way around my rectum. When I wake up next, somebody has decided it's time to roll me back to my shadowy room on the second floor of the hospital. My funky little air mattress feels like quicksand, but I'm too weak to move or protest anyway.

(Side note: Today's hospitals use fancy, advanced, mechanical air mattresses for their beds, apparently to help prevent bedsores. The result is a very uncomfortable, constantly moving, quicksand-like contraption that makes you feel like you are always about to drown. Imagine if manic claustrophobia married the deep end of the ocean. Their love child would be the hospital bed I spent nearly a week in.)

When I wake up on my birthday, December 10, I feel like I can't remember what it's like to move my arms or legs.

(Another side note: For two or three days, every time I woke up, it was a brand-new shock to me that I was in the hospital, that I was suffering in surprisingly great pain, and that I hadn't simply gotten an antibiotic prescription when I went to the doctor. I guess I'm a slow learner.)

Breathing hurts, as does something simple like lifting my head or rolling over on my side. I'm aware that my left hand cradles a little button. When I push the button, it flushes pain medicine into my veins. Apparently, I pushed that button 38 times the day before—enough to trigger an allergic reaction. I'm tempted to ignore the fact that my entire body is now itching as well as dying (or something like dying), but then my lips go numb and my tongue starts to tingle. I figure I better tell somebody. They give me Benadryl and suggest maybe I should go a little easier on the pain-relief switch. Sigh.

The next several days are a blur of malnutrition (anesthesia causes your bowels to go dormant, and they can't let you eat or drink until your bowel "wakes up." Sound familiar?), deprivation, vomiting, inescapable pain, constant nauseating smells, and (you may not believe this, but it's true) occasional, too-brief, white-hot moments of Christ's Holy Spirit whispering strength and comfort into my bewildered soul. I found myself just begging him to let me worship, because in those moments, all too short, brought unexpected relief and peace. Every time I was tempted to forget he was near, he forced his way back into my awareness. Finally I figured, *Well, heck, if he's not going away, I guess that means I'll just have to hang on and finish this ride after all*. But mostly I kept thinking about Amy.

I really missed my wife.

I think that's what hurt the most. I just missed my girl. But she was in the nadir of her chemotherapy and couldn't risk the exposure of coming to the hospital to see me. In fact, I demanded that she stay away and would have been VERY angry had she even tried to risk coming to see me. But even still, I cried for her more than I care to admit. My nurses were very patient and compassionate through all my tears. They were the same ones who had ministered to Amy just weeks before, so they knew what I was missing.

I don't really remember visitors coming into or leaving my room, but I remember seeing people suddenly appear and disappear from time to time. Jimmy came by to check on me. My brother-in-law Erik Brolsma came a few times too. (Sorry if I was talking nonsense, Erik!) So did Jennifer, Colleen, and others. I have no idea really who came and who didn't, but the best moment was when my father-in-law showed up out of nowhere. (Norm? Aren't you in Phoenix right now? Never mind, things don't have to make sense yet.) He pulled me out of my quicksand bed and faced me toward the window. And there was my girl, standing safely on the sidewalk below, waving and crying and calling me on my cell phone. That was good medicine, except for the headache and clogged nose I had from sobbing so hard at the sight of her tiny little frame dancing a jig to prove to me she was doing OK and that you all were taking very good care of her.

At some point in those blurry days, Nurse Tim stopped by to check on me. He was a cheery guy, and we reminisced briefly about our time in the foxhole together. Then he got this sincere look on his face and he said to me, "I have to tell you…"

"Yeah?" I said, and I'm thinking, *Man, this guy and I have been through hell and back together. I wonder what he's got to say about that.*

And he looks at me earnestly and says, "You are the hairiest person I have ever seen."

Huh.

I want to make some smart retort like, "Yeah, but you've never seen my mother," but I know that's unfair to Mom, and well, I'm pretty sure I am the hairiest person I've ever seen too. So finally I decide just to own it.

"Yeah," I say, "at least I've got that going for me." Best I could do in the circumstances. Sorry.

And the days grind into more days. I find myself giving myself the same lectures I've been giving to Amy: "You won't always feel like you feel right now." "You can trust God to help you trust God." "Time is part of the prescription." It actually helps. Go figure. I start walking the halls, trying to, um, get things moving, as they say in the neighborhood, but one day I walk down a hall and suddenly think maybe I'm going to pass out. I find a chair and wait awhile. A guy pushes a wheelchair past me and disappears. About 15 minutes later, he reappears, and so I muster my courage.

"Excuse me," I say meekly, "could you help me get back to my room?"

He is kind enough to load me into his wheelchair and shove me back to my room, where the nurses are starting to sweat about my prolonged absence. For some reason, after that I'm no longer allowed to leave my room without an escort.

And finally there is the not-so-sweet smell of success in the toilet of my room, and on December 14 I am at last freed from the claustrophobia of the quicksand bed. My father-in-law, who is definitely not in Phoenix now (thank you, Norm!), chauffeurs me back to my little yellow house with a white picket fence, decorated in the beauty of holiday snow. I hurt all over. I have a new life ahead of me that will apparently include regular IV infusions and monthly vitamin shots. I've lost 35 pounds and now weigh about what I did when I was in eighth grade. I may have finally met the thing that will eventually kill me. I may get better; I may get worse. Only God knows. I can barely breathe while I'm walking from my driveway into my garage, like my chest just won't fill with air. But when I make that short trip across the pavement, I see that my girl is waiting for me by the door.

And she's wearing the hugging shirt.

Wednesday, December 30, 2015

So for my birthday, a friend gave me an eBay gift card, which of course means "Time for Mikey to buy more useless comics." Believe it or not, I'm seriously considering laying out $10 for an old beat-up comic titled "Captain America Meets the Asthma Monster." (I know it makes no sense. Just go with it.) Still, the comic I'd really like to buy is one that Stan Lee has yet to write: "Captain America Kicks the Cancer Monster in the Nether Regions and Then Laughs When the Monster Says Bad Words, Shrivels Up, and Dies While Writhing on the Pavement."

Sadly, that comic still hasn't been put on the agenda for a publishing committee meeting over at Marvel Entertainment. Whatever. Since I can't get a Cap / Cancer Monster comic on eBay, perhaps you'd be willing to toss out the next best thing on Facebook?

Tomorrow (December 31) is another chemotherapy day for our girl. How about if we give her a "Mickey Mouse against Cancer" day? Would you be willing to wear some kind of Mickey accessory or apparel and use that as a reminder to pray for Amy and her medical treatment tomorrow? And hey, if you want to post pictures on Facebook, we wouldn't object.

Thanks, loved ones! You are all a great encouragement to us—thanks for sticking around for the long, bumpy ride. We look forward to your prayers!

Thursday, December 31, 2015

(From Amy!)

Hi, everyone! Chemo 5 is done! Everything went well, and I'm feeling good. I expect to feel tired and beaten up a bit over the next few days and then hope to rebound to feeling energetic again. The doctor said I'm doing great. She seemed really pleased with my weight and energy level and body functions and all that. She even released me for a few more hours a week at work—yay!

Thanks for all the fun posts you made today. I was a bit nervous as I headed to the chemo treatment today, and those posts gave me a lot of encouragement. Having so many friends pray me through this has made such a difference. When I found out I had cancer, I knew right away that "my people" were going to be an important part of my healing—I knew I would not be able to go this alone or in private.

Sometimes things have been a bit more "open" than I imagined they would be, especially when I first discovered I had cancer. (Yes, I'm referring to all the posts about pooping and passing gas. Who would ever think this would be part of what you would share with your friends?) But knowing you all are with Mike and me on this journey makes all the difference in the world.

I am now completely off the IV nutrition and am eating normal foods again. What a delight to eat a sandwich or a slice of pizza! What a delight to chew food! I am off all pain medicines and am only taking vitamins and similar supplements. I am amazed at what God is doing in my body—and how God continues to provide encouragement for Mike and me when we feel like we can't take the next step.

Thank you, thank you, thank you!

Sunday, January 3, 2016

The good news at the start of 2016 is that chemotherapy seems to be working! According to our doctor, Amy is progressing very well, and her body is responding as hoped to the treatments. Our doctor believes our girl is out of the danger zone and well on the road to recovery. Thank you, Jesus!

The bad news is that chemotherapy is just tough on a person's body. Amy is no exception. There is a cumulative effect that seems to hit Amy harder with each new treatment, sooo…Amy is back on nausea medicine, at least for now. It just wasn't realistic for her to stay off it at this point. She hasn't needed pain medicine this time around, so that's good, but she's been kind of beat up this whole weekend—feeling run down, weak, and just generally uncomfortable.

Bonus: With her weakened immune system and despite our best efforts, she caught a cold over the holidays, which just makes everything a little bit harder. She doesn't have much of an appetite, so eating is a chore. It's hard to keep up her strength as the day goes on. I'm still not up to full strength either (sheesh, will I ever again be able to lift a gallon of milk without wincing?), so all that is to say it's been kind of a tiring weekend. (Fortunately, a friend loaned us *Frasier* season 1, so we've just been slugs in front of the TV screen, which has been good medicine.)

Anyway, tonight before bed, I saw a handwritten note that's been on my refrigerator since August 19. On that morning, just before her sister drove her to the hospital for surgery, Amy left the note for me to find. It said only this:

"My hope is built on nothing less
 than Jesus' blood and righteousness."[2]

Moments before the scariest experience of her life, that's what was on our girl's mind, and that's what she wanted me to know. I put the note on my refrigerator way back then and have read it every day since.

---

2. Edward Mote, "My Hope Is Built on Nothing Less," 1834.

I saw Amy's note again tonight just before bed, just when I was feeling exhausted and helpless. I had to stop and read it a few times because it suddenly struck me how true those words have been these past five months. Right now I'm still exhausted, weak, and a little sore, but at least the weight of the weekend has been lifted off my shoulders. I do not have to hope in these circumstances or lose hope when this situation is more difficult than I wanted it to be. My hope rests where it's safe, in Jesus himself, regardless of what this world does or doesn't do for me. This was comforting news on August 19, and is still a comfort today, on January 3.

So tonight Amy and I are both tired, a little beat up…and filled with hope for tomorrow. God is always good. (I think you probably knew that already, but I figured it couldn't hurt to remind you.)

Thank you for steadfastly keeping us in your prayers, especially in the coming days. We need you more than you know and are grateful to have you in our lives. We love you!

Thursday, January 7, 2016

(From Amy!)

Hi, everyone! A short update: I am doing much better now—past the worst of the chemo crud. Eating normally again, and my energy has returned. Yay!

I do have a prayer request for you prayer warriors. Mike is still healing from his surgery. It's slow, but he is improving. Tomorrow he goes for his second infusion of Remicade, which will start helping the Crohn's symptoms. He's a bit apprehensive about going—it takes about two and a half hours on the IV. Last time he didn't have any of the negative side effects, so we are praying he will not have any again this time. I know many of you wear Mickey on my chemo days to show support and to remind you to pray for me. If anyone wants to don a cape or other superhero apparel tomorrow to remind you to pray for Mike, that would be awesome! (If you do wear a cape, please take a picture—I'd really want to make sure the whole world saw that!)

Love you all! Thanks for cheering us along this journey!

Tuesday, January 12, 2016

(From Amy!)

Happy Tuesday, everyone! It's sunny here today, and we are thankful for that!

Mike did fine during his Remicade infusion last week (and we loved all the cape photos!), but since then he has had one side effect after another. Some of them went away within 24 hours, but he has had a lot of severe pain in his hands and arms. It turns out this is one of the rare side effects. (Of course, we are very special in this house, and that's why we get the rare side effects!) He got a prescription for a steroid today and will pick that up this afternoon—we are hoping it will make a difference in the pain.

Thanks for praying for us—we sure appreciate your conversations with God that include a mention of us!

Tuesday, January 12, 2016

Quick update: I am having a lot of pain today in my arms and my right hand. It appears to be a very rare (less than 1 percent) side effect of the Remicade infusion. I can barely use my right hand—can't even open a medicine bottle or unzip my pants and can't raise my arms much higher than my chest. The condition came on fast and hard last night. I feel like an invalid, and poor Amy is having to do things like help me get dressed and get food. The doctor has prescribed a steroid for treatment, and we'll have to figure out how to avoid this happening next time. For now, though, we would really appreciate your prayers. It's hard for a writer to get anything done without the use of his hands. We love you! Thank you!

Wednesday, January 13, 2016

Dang. Last fall I contracted to start a new online entertainment column on January 1 for a large Christian website. For obvious reasons, I was unable to do that, so when I was in the hospital I asked for an extension of the start date so I could recover. Well, they notified me today that since I missed the January 1 date, they are canceling my contract rather than waiting for me to get well enough to write the column. Pray that I am able to handle this disappointment with grace and kindness even though it kind of pisses me off. Dang.

On the bright side, my left hand is completely back to normal, my rotator cuffs in both shoulders are working again, and my right hand is improving (just not as quickly as the other hand). So THANKS SO MUCH for your prayers yesterday. It was kind of scary to feel suddenly paralyzed for an extended period. But God is good, as usual, and except for the stupid contract cancelation, I'm feeling much better today.

Sometime soon I'll also update you on Amy—after all, this is supposed to be her group, not a place for my constant whining, right?

Love you all!

Friday, January 15, 2016

(From Amy!)

My hair is starting to grow back! I have my last chemo coming up on January 28—but my hair has already started sprouting. I can't stop rubbing it!

And thanks to everyone for praying for Mike. He is doing SO much better!

Wednesday, January 20, 2016

(From Amy!)

One little spot on my arm is all that's left to show from my five months of having a PICC line. I have to say I like not having two ports coming out of my arm. Today I took a shower without having someone wrap my arm in plastic. Making progress!

4

Ring the Bell

For the LORD is good and his love endures forever;
his faithfulness continues through all generations.

PSALM 100:5

Thursday, January 21, 2016

Every so often at the Cancer Center, you'll hear a bell ring and people cheering. No, it's not because an angel got its wings (sorry, Frank Capra). It means that one special cancer survivor has finished the long, cruel, grueling cycle of chemotherapy or radiation treatment. It means (God willing) the worst is behind and the best is yet to come. It signals victory and a return to a cancer-free life, at least for the time being. When a cancer patient finishes that last infusion, when all the needles and IV bags are packed away in the hazard bin, the patient gets to grab that bell and ring it with all the gusto he or she has. It's a simple little ceremony that announces to the world (well, at least to the Cancer Center inhabitants) "I am alive! I am…ALIVE!"

This is the bell that waits for us in the Cancer Center. A week from today, Amy will ring it and walk out the doors into her brand-new life.

In case you didn't know it already, God is good.

Tuesday, January 26, 2016

(From Amy!)

Hello, friends! The countdown is on! I have to admit I'm a little nervous about heading to my last chemo on Thursday. Will my blood markers be OK? Will this really be the end of it? Will there be more tests? Will the cancer be gone? Will I be able to go back to "normal" life soon? Lots of things that I don't know. Of course, God does know, and that gives me some comfort—none of this surprises him. Have to keep trusting that I am in his hands. Thanks for keeping me in your prayers! I really am looking forward to ringing that bell—will be sure to get a picture of that moment!

Thursday, January 28, 2016

(From Amy!)

Come on, ring that bell! Thank you, Jesus—God is good!

Tuesday, February 2, 2016

(From Amy!)

Tomorrow will be a banner day in our home—and we want to invite you to pray and celebrate with us.

First, I have been given permission to actually GO to work tomorrow! When I first was diagnosed with cancer, they told me I would be out for six weeks. That was six months ago! There have been many setbacks along the way, but the doctor says I am now strong enough to be back at Group. I have to wear a mask for a couple of weeks, but getting that clearance letter from the doctor feels like a miracle!

Second, Mike has his next Remicade infusion tomorrow. You likely all remember that the last time he had every possible side effect and was in a lot of pain. This time they are taking precautions with new medications being added in, but Mike is anxious about the whole thing, so prayers are appreciated!

Finally, my wonderful mom is flying out here tomorrow to warm our home with her loving touch and to help us. While we are making great progress, we still need a bit of extra care. With all the snow, we would be grateful for prayers for her safe travel.

Thank you all! We love you!

Wednesday, February 3, 2016

(From Amy!)

Me ready for work. Mike ready for infusion. It's a new day!

Later…

So I scared my nurses today during the Remicade infusion. I had an allergic reaction that didn't feel all that serious to me but that made them jump into action and get the EpiPen ready in case I stopped breathing. They cut short the infusion and then insisted on watching me for more than an hour, taking my blood pressure and temperature every five minutes. I felt fine after about half an hour, just tired, but they refused to let me leave until they were sure I wasn't going to quit breathing. God was good—I'm still breathing!

Long story short, I failed the Remicade test, so we're back to square one for treatment, which postpones my recovery schedule again (dang). My doctor is lobbying my insurance to approve a different treatment (I'll have to give myself a shot every two weeks for the rest of my life) that will, we hope, get me back on the road to recovery. We'll see how it goes.

Meanwhile, thanks for your prayers! I'm worn out and my hands are stiff and sore, but I'm otherwise unharmed from today's experience. I expect I'll sleep well tonight.

When you and Jesus are talking this evening, please thank him for his kindness and mention my new need as part of your conversation. Thank you. We love you!

Sunday, February 7, 2016

Just over two weeks ago, we were sitting in the Cancer Center waiting to have the dressing changed on Amy's PICC line when one of her "chemo buddies" walked through and stopped to chat with us. Over the past six months, Shirley and Amy had often endured chemotherapy sessions together and chatted together on Facebook. In fact, this group is how they met! Shirley was in good spirits while she talked with us, upbeat and energetic. She was heading to her last radiation treatment, she said. She felt good and looked good. She, like us, could finally see the finish line of this awful cancer thing. She took time to encourage our girl with the hope of God's goodness and faithfulness and mentioned she'd be praying as Amy prepared to "ring her bell" the next week. She walked away with a little bounce in her step, smiling.

That was the last time we saw her.

Shirley had a setback, went into hospice this past week, and then slipped into Jesus's loving arms yesterday. It was just barely two weeks.

I'm thinking of Shirley and her family this Sunday morning, and I'm struck by the way God's mercy enacts itself in our lives. These two women sat side by side through suffering in hope of healing. Amy's mercy, it appears, has been given in physical recovery; Shirley's mercy was given in physical release. I don't know why Christ's one mercy shows itself in two different ways like this, but I do know that God has been present in both circumstances. I've seen the strokes of our Artist's paintbrush in each of these women's lives.

We have one more month to wait before we find out if Amy's cancer has gone into remission—to see how God's mercy will finally play out in this time in our lives. We know that some beat cancer and live long lives afterward and some don't. No one is ever promised tomorrow. Whatever happens, we'll take comfort in Shirley's encouragement and example. God is good and faithful, she said, and she's right. He is always good.

Please remember to pray for Shirley's family in this time of loss.

"I know whom I have believed, and am convinced that he is able to guard what I have entrusted to him until that day" (2 Timothy 1:12).

Tuesday, February 9, 2016

So even with wearing a mask and using copious amounts of Purell, our girl has already caught the beginnings of a cold. Sigh. Please pray that she'll be able to maintain strength and health and get enough rest during this nadir week and be returned to full health soon. Thank you!

Friday, February 12, 2016

Tonight ends Amy's last nadir period. To celebrate, we are retiring (and cleaning) the Hugging Shirt! Woo-hoo!

Monday, February 15, 2016

Another of Amy's chemo buddies has been moved to hospice. Our hearts are heavy.

Zoe made it her business to cheer Amy from the beginning, way back in August, visiting Amy in the ICU and offering encouragement and kindness every time we saw her. She often brought her keyboard into the Cancer Center to play comforting music while Amy and others endured treatment. She had been in remission, and we were surprised to see her with an IV hooked up to her one day as Amy neared the bell-ringing day. Zoe maintained a positive attitude but eventually discontinued the chemotherapy. She is suffering now, and the end is near.

When you're speaking with Jesus today, will you mention Zoe? Please thank him for her kindness to us and ask him to ease her suffering with his own kindness. Zoe will be missed.

Saturday, February 20, 2016

(From Amy!)

So many wonderful milestones in the past couple of weeks.

My mom was here for two weeks, and I got to hug her as much as I wanted!

I have been able to be at work without a mask—so good to be there!

Got to hold my new grandson, Cayde Nappa! There was a time when I didn't know if I would live to meet him. What joy!

Have cuddled and snuggled with my granddaughter, Genevieve Nappa, singing songs with her in bed, and watched her sing on stage at VBS.

Went to coffee with my friend Lisa. We talked, laughed, and cried a whole bunch.

Ate pizza with my best friend, Jennifer Hanes, and loved being with her.

These are just a few of my miracle moments. So many more in the past few weeks. God is so good. I am so thankful!

Wednesday, February 24, 2016

(From Amy!)

I keep having wonderful days! Have been able to be back at church, have gone to the gym, and have eaten out at a restaurant. Best of all are the hugs and time I am getting to spend with family and friends. I feel amazed every day!

Today I go in to have blood drawn, and tomorrow Mike and I will meet with the oncologist to see where I am in the battle. I realize it is possible she will say that the cancer is still there and I will have to face new treatments, but I am praying that she says I am in remission and don't have to go back for any tests for three months. Feel free to pray about that!

Thursday, February 25, 2016

(From Amy!)

Hello, friends!

I just got back from seeing the oncologist. I had blood drawn yesterday, and she went over the results with me today. For the marker she is looking at, under 35 is normal. My number today is 21! (To give you perspective, when I first found out I had cancer, it was over 3,400!) So this is a day of rejoicing!

I don't have to go back to the doctor for three months—wahoo! Thank you all for your prayers and words of encouragement! I have needed every bit of it!

Tuesday, April 12, 2016

(From Amy!)

Hello, my friends!

It's been more than a month since I posted—no news is good news! But I thought some of you might like an update. I went today for a "survivor" appointment at the doctor's office. They reviewed my history from my first appointment until where I am today and talked about long-term side effects I have ahead of me. A few things to share.

First, they reviewed my original diagnosis. When Mike and I first met with the oncologist the day before my surgery last August, she said she believed my cancer was stage III-C—so pretty bad. But after surgery they changed it to stage IV-B—even worse! It is incredible to think my situation was so dire. Makes me even more thankful to be alive today. God has brought me so far!

Second, we talked about my situation today. On one hand, I am doing great. Everything related to cancer is under control. But a side effect of the chemo is ongoing muscle pain. I am trying a variety of things to manage this (hot baths, yoga, a variety of vitamins and supplements, and so on), but I would definitely appreciate your prayers. The pain tends to be worst in the late evening and at night when I am trying to sleep. They say I can expect this to last up to a year from my last chemo. But it's a small price to pay, considering the other option!

Again, thank you all for your love and support of Mike and me. We are so grateful! I can't imagine being on this journey without such amazing and loving cheerleaders!

5

Maybe It's Pneumonia...

Let me hear of your unfailing love each morning,
for I am trusting you.
Show me where to walk,
for I give myself to you.

PSALM 143:8 NLT

Friday, April 29, 2016

All right, so here's an unexpected surprise. Amy has had a bad cold for about a week. She went to the doctor today, thinking it might be turning into something worse. They took X-rays and it turns out she has "pleural effusion"—liquid in the lining of her lungs.

Causes? Could be caused by pneumonia...or cancer. Sigh.

We're not sure what's next at this point. Amy is resting, and we are waiting to hear from the oncologist's office. She's a little somber but at peace. We'll know what we know when we know, I guess.

Feel free to lift us up in your prayers today!

Later...

Off to the Cancer Center to have fluid drained and sent out for testing to determine if there are any cancer cells in it. Thank you for your prayers!

Later...

All right, we are back from the ER. The news is not good, but at least we are all home and together in a cozy house filled with love.

They stuck a large needle in Amy's back and drained two liters of fluid out of her lungs, but they had to stop before draining it all because Amy passed out (well, almost passed out), and it was making her too weak. There was also concern of creating a blood clot, so they left about one liter still sloshing inside the lining of her lungs. They said she will probably have to go back and have it drained again unless the antibiotic helps her body fight it and reabsorb the fluid.

Amy's doctor in the emergency room was an old acquaintance of ours from our previous church, so that was nice. She said to him, "Maybe it's just pneumonia," and he shook his head and said, "It's not pneumonia." Apparently this fluid buildup in her lungs is similar to the ascites fluid that built up in her abdomen when we first discovered cancer. Of course, until the test results come back next week (Monday or Tuesday), we can't confirm the doctor's opinion, but signs point that way. They took four vials of blood and (obviously) quite a bit of fluid for testing. We'll let you know results when we know.

Our girl is maintaining good spirits, though she's in quite a bit of pain from the day's ordeal. Pray for her to be able to rest, for her body to begin absorbing fluid left in her lungs, and for God to prevent her body from making new fluid inside her.

No idea what this means for the long haul or even what the next steps will be. We'll worry about that when the time comes. Meanwhile, God is always good. We love you!

Saturday, April 30, 2016

(From Amy!)

Hello, my dear friends! Thank you much for your prayers and love! Yesterday was rough, but I slept so well last night (finally able to breathe!), and today I was able to go out for coffee with my dad and run a few errands. Thankful for a bit of energy.

Don't know what will be ahead…but for today, I am grateful.

Love to you all!

Sunday, May 1, 2016

Amy is doing well today. She says her right side is sore, but otherwise she feels good. This will surprise no one: She is planning to go to work tomorrow morning.

About ten zillion people (give or take) gathered around us to pray this morning. It was kind of claustrophobic but also very nice to be loved. Very nice.

We should have more news on the situation soon. Until then we are hoping for the best yet preparing for the worst. Regardless of what is, this is what we know: God is good. He is always good, and we are very grateful. We love you!

Monday, May 2, 2016

Hello, loved ones,

At this point you've loved us through hell and back, so I guess there's no reason to be coy about things.

Yesterday Amy and I stopped by Target and bought her a pretty little notebook. She said she wanted to write down some thoughts that included messages for a few loved ones as well as funeral preferences. She spent a good part of the afternoon scribbling quietly in that book. When she was done, she looked happy. Subdued and sober, but happy. Afterward, she ate a full meal for the first time in three days (thanks for the soup, Brooke!)—I think just because it was emotionally therapeutic for her to finally be able to stare mortality in the face and say, "I'm not afraid of you." We both felt better.

Later, some of her friends reprimanded her for buying that precious notebook, saying, "It's like you're giving up!" I was heartbroken and angry when I heard they'd treated her with that kind of insensitivity and harshness. "It's OK," Amy told me, calming me down. "They don't understand. They are my friends, and they're scared. It's OK."

We had a quiet evening reading, listening to music, just being together. It was nice. Amy slept reasonably well last night and got up for work this morning. She was sick for a bit at first but grateful "it was only dry heaves." I asked her to stay home, to call in sick, and you can imagine the eye-roll she gave me. She did at least lie down until her stomach settled. Then she went in to work. (As usual. This girl loves her job, right? I think she mostly loves just being with her coworkers, which says a lot about them.)

She talked to the nurse at the oncologist's office this morning, and the nurse told her she wouldn't get results of tests until tomorrow. Then about an hour later the oncologist called unexpectedly. (Our regular oncologist is out on maternity leave, so this doctor is her partner—we like him.) He couldn't tell me specifics, but he did say, "I'm going to need both you and Amy to come in to see me."

We all know what that means, right?

Amy talked to him a few minutes later, and it is what we suspected. The cancer has returned in force. That it could do so only two months after the completion of chemotherapy shows how aggressive stage IV-B cancer is. We were supposed to get about three years before this kind of thing happened; we got fewer than two months. At any rate, the normal cancer marker rate is anywhere from 0 to 35. At February's end, Amy's marker was a beautiful 21. By the end of April it was 659. Right now it continues to rise, signaling the spread inside of Amy's body. Sigh.

So we have an appointment tomorrow at 3:00 p.m. to "go over options" with the oncologist. From where we sit, none of the options look good. This is the way it is sometimes.

We love you all, so we must be honest with you. Sometimes bad cancer kills good people. No, we haven't given up (and no need to lecture us on that, OK folks?), but we are also certain that no one lives forever on this earth. That's reserved for our time with Jesus in eternity. Yes, Jesus can heal, and yes, we are asking him to heal. But we also know that just because Jesus can heal doesn't mean we are entitled to his healing. His strength is made perfect in our weakness. Jesus is generous, and sometimes his generosity is displayed in ways that are different from our expectations. That's OK. It's healthy, even.

And please know that while God's goodness can always be seen in our circumstances, our circumstances are not the definition of God's goodness. We are too nearsighted for that, too remedial in our understanding of truth and the way God is working in our lives.

We are very aware of Christ's calming closeness today. We would wish for healing, but his presence is really all that we need—now and forever. Thank you for your prayers on our behalf.

We love you!

Tuesday, May 3, 2016

(From Amy!)

Hello, everyone!

I am going to say that I have good news. No, the cancer is not gone. But… there is a treatment plan, and I can get started on it quickly. That is hugely encouraging to me!

They do know I have cancer in the lining around my lungs. It may be other places too, but that will not change the treatment plan, so I am not going to have a scan.

The plan at this moment is that tomorrow I will have a test on my heart to make sure I can tolerate more chemo. Then I will start chemo on Thursday using an IV instead of a port. Then I will get a port put in next week for ongoing chemo treatments, which at this point will be every three weeks.

They are going to have to drain the fluid from my chest at least one more time, but the hope is that starting chemo sooner rather than later will stop that fluid from building up. Not fun, but necessary.

We are going to consult with another doctor after I start chemo, and there are conversations about the best batch of drugs to use, but we do have one in mind to start with.

The outlook without this treatment is super grim—three months at best. And the reality is that there is no guarantee this treatment will work. But the doctor thinks it should work, and we're going to give it a try. Another bit of good news is that I get to keep working as long as I am strong enough. Yay!

I can't even BEGIN to tell you how much all your prayers and hugs and notes and all have meant to us in the past few days. Just overwhelming. I told someone today I feel like I'm crowd-surfing on the prayers of everyone. You are holding us up!

More posts to come as we learn more. Do pray that the test on my heart goes well and that I will still be considered a good candidate for chemo.

I LOVE YOU!

Wednesday, May 4, 2016

(From Amy!)

Hello, dear friends!

I am scheduled for chemo at 2:00 p.m. on Thursday. If you're willing, wear something Mickey Mouse as a reminder to pray for me. We will update when it's over. Love-love-love you all!

Thursday, May 5, 2016

(From Amy!)

Just got home from chemo. All went well. Breezy, Mike, and Jeanne all kept me company, and Jeanne brought guacamole for us to snack on while the infusion was going. I expect to feel OK for the next day or so. Then I should crash over the weekend. All part of the cycle. Thank you all for praying for me. I am thankful everything went smoothly. Your love and prayers have been a huge encouragement to me!

Tuesday, May 10, 2016

We are back in the hospital with severe abdominal pain and vomiting. Early indications seem to be another bowel blockage caused by the cancer. Please love us in your prayers. Thank you.

Later...

OK, thanks for your patience. This is going to be a long post, but let's see if I can get everyone up to date. If you're short on time, the last paragraph here is the most important one, so just skip to there and you'll be fine.

1. Two weeks ago, we found out that (a) Amy's cancer has returned, and (b) it is angry. When Amy entered remission in February, doctors were very optimistic. They figured that she should stay cancer-free for at least three years and that if she could stay in remission five years, she could beat the disease long-term. Well, we got only about two months before we discovered the cancer had reappeared, meaning it probably came back within a month or so, and we didn't discover it until Amy started having complications from it. Our current oncologist (our regular doctor is on maternity leave) called this "unusually aggressive" for cancer, considering the treatment Amy had endured to make it go away.

2. This is the part with the bad news. If you don't like bad news, skip this paragraph. The cancer is terminal. This is the thing that will end Amy's life. Untreated, our oncologist estimates she would have fewer than 90 days to live. So we are now entering the phase he calls "buying time." He thinks with new chemotherapy infusions followed by oral chemotherapy maintenance drugs, he can realistically "buy" about three years. If everything goes better than expected, maybe five years. He encouraged me to make sure the time Amy has remaining is "quality years." I'm not sure what that means yet, but I'm going to do it anyway. Regardless, our girl now comes with an expiration date. We are still learning to deal with that. Gratefully, we have found Jesus nearby to help us.

3. Yes, Amy plans to work pretty much until she drops dead at her desk. Just warning you folks at Group Publishing. Our girl is not going to let a little thing like cancer keep her from the office.

4. Here's the current plan:

(a) Four to six more chemotherapy infusions over the next several months. This is a little difficult because Amy has already burned through three chemo medications, so the options for chemo drugs have dwindled. But there is a fourth drug the oncologist thinks will work, so we have begun that. If it works, we move to the next step. If it doesn't work, we begin thinking about "quality days" instead of "quality years." Still, we are optimistic it will work and lead us to…

(b) Oral chemotherapy drug to stave off an "aggressive" return of cancer. We keep doing this as long as it is effective, hopefully for at least three years, maybe five years…who knows? God can do whatever he wants to do with Amy's life, so we just have to wait and see what he chooses to do. Meantime, we are going to see what it's really like to "live like you're dying." Should be interesting.

(c) We take Amy to Disneyland in September. (First step in making "quality years" for our girl, right?)

(d) At some point, when the oral chemo loses effectiveness, we begin to watch Amy, well, "pack for eternity." We are praying she will be made comfortable and pain-free when the time comes.

(e) Then we have a big party where we all cry and laugh and thank Jesus for giving us the privilege of having Amy in our lives.

5. Of course, it's always possible God will overrule that plan and wipe out cancer in a miracle of healing, and we save the big party for decades from now. We're OK with that. But honestly, whatever God decides in this situation will be the right decision. We trust him.

6. We are in the hospital right now with complications from the current angry cancer. Amy is suffering a new bowel blockage (time to pray for intestinal perfume, please) and fluid buildup between the linings of her lungs. They are planning a minor, out-patient-style surgery for tomorrow to give her a line so she can drain the fluid at home in the future and to also install a permanent port to make chemotherapy infusions easier. God willing, we expect her to go home tomorrow night.

7. We are concerned about nutrition, so we need this bowel blockage to clear. (Time to fight on your knees, friends. You know what to do.) They say if we can get through the second chemotherapy—in about two weeks—that should help prevent future bowel blockages, so we just need to make sure Amy is able to eat between now and then.

All right, I think that brings you up to date.

Thank you for walking so faithfully beside us during this time! You are Christ's hands and heart in our lives, and we are grateful for you.

Ready…set…pray!

Later…

OK, so I'm looking at my last post, and I've decided I'm tired of being sad and making everyone else sad with me. So before I go to sleep tonight, let me tell you a few stories to help us all feel a little better.

Story #1

Before I left the hospital tonight, my girl said to me, "You need a haircut." Challenge accepted! I came home and quickly unearthed my trusty electric razor. I stood in front of the mirror in my bathroom…and then…I did a *fine job* cutting my own hair. (What? You were expecting something different? Ahem.)[1]

Story #2

Amy left the ER and was admitted into a regular hospital room at about 2:00 a.m. this morning. Three nurses were working the night shift on the second floor when we got there. They are kind women who have cared for Amy previously. I don't know if anyone else on the second floor needed an RN's help at 2:00 a.m. last night, but if they did, they didn't get it because all three of those nurses were packed into Amy's room to greet her when she arrived.

And apparently there was a minor dispute over which one would get to be Amy's night nurse. A nurse had been assigned Amy by the luck of the draw, but

---

1. OK, yes, back in November my head did have a mishap with an electric razor. But sometimes it's best to keep the bald-headed past in the past, no?

she had the least seniority. She was quickly replaced by a nurse with a higher rank who wanted to personally make sure Amy was well cared for. The third nurse lost out on the Amy lottery but ended up spending about half an hour with Amy anyway, making sure she was comfortable, chatting, and kind of ignoring her own patients just to make time for our girl. So you know, if you have to go to the hospital in the near future, you might want to call ahead and make sure Amy's not there. Otherwise there might be a nurse shortage on the night shift.

Story #3

In the mythology of oncology, there is a beast commonly known as "Chemo Brain." This is the excuse every cancer patient uses for flubbing something simple, for being plagued by absentmindedness, or for just plain forgetting the obvious. It seems that Amy had a Chemo Brain sighting recently…

Our heroine was hard at work when the doctor's office called and left a message about scheduling some sort of something. Amy dutifully took notes, writing down several phone numbers so she wouldn't forget them. Then at the earliest opportunity, she sat down at her desk to return the call.

While she was waiting for the doctor's office to answer, her cell phone rang in her purse. *Dang*, she thought. *I better get it because maybe the nurse is calling me again*. She ended her call and fished out her cell phone. Just as she answered the cell, the person on the other end hung up. *How annoying*, she thought.

She redialed the doctor's office and, while she was waiting for an answer, wouldn't you know it? Her cell phone rang again. She checked the caller ID and saw it was a Group Publishing number, which likely meant that someone on her team needed immediate help with a problem. Amy has her priorities straight: The people she supervises are always at the top of her list. So she reached for her cell and hung up again on the doctor's office. Alas, she'd waited too long to answer, and just missed the person calling her.

Now she was flustered and mildly irritated, but she had to get that medical something-or-other scheduled, so she called the doctor again. You guessed it, her cell phone rang again. This time Amy decided just to let the caller leave a message, thinking she'd call that person back after taking care of business with the doctor. Meanwhile, the receptionists at the doctor's office were taking longer than usual to answer their phone. Finally Amy's call dumped into voice mail, and she heard a cheerful voice saying in her ear, "You've reached Amy Nappa. I'm away from my phone right now..."

She looked again at the number she'd dialed and suddenly realized the truth: It was her own cell phone. She'd written it down to remind herself to give it to the doctor's office—and then called herself *three times* before she realized what she was doing.

That, dear friends, is proof the Chemo Brain really does exist. At least that's Amy's story (and she's sticking to it!).

We love you!

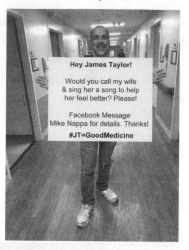

Wednesday, May 11, 2016

So here's the thing: Amy says the only regret she has in life (besides cancer) is that she never saw James Taylor live in concert. It doesn't look like she ever will, so I started wishing, *Wouldn't it be cool if JT were to call her and sing her favorite song on the phone?* Then I decided, *Why not? I'm going to ask him if he'll do that!* Then I started thinking, *What if WE ALL asked him to do that? What if hundreds of us asked James Taylor to sing a song for Amy—would he do it?* I say let's find out.

Will you join with me and post this request on James Taylor's Facebook page and also ask your friends and churches and coworkers and family members to do the same? Is it possible for us to get a few hundred people to relay this message to James Taylor? Would he respond? It might be fun to see what happens…

Thank you!

Later…

All right, they are taking Amy into surgery right now. We'd love your prayers for Amy today—thank you!

They say it's just a minor surgery (they are installing the chemotherapy port and putting a catheter into her lung to make it easier to drain fluid in the future) and that our girl will be up and running by tomorrow. Of course, she's taking that to mean "You can work a full day without restrictions tomorrow." My guess is that it might be next week before she can do that, but hey, she does what she wants to do, doesn't she?

Anesthesia can interfere with bowel function, so when you are praying, please pray specifically that God will spare Amy that side effect. She's eaten nothing for about two days now, and we need her to eat so she can maintain strength enough for her next chemotherapy infusion on May 26.

Thank you! We love you!

Later…

Here's the latest.

Amy is out of surgery and in the recovery room. The doctor says she did fine during the surgery but that her lung is partially collapsed from all the fluid built up in there. They couldn't completely uncollapse (is that a word?) the lung, so they left it in hopes it will expand and return to function on its own. (Add that to your prayer lists, folks—thanks!)

She will be in the recovery area for about an hour, with the hope of returning her to her hospital room around 2:00-ish. Big concern, obviously, is still the bowel blockage. Please pray that the anesthesia does not slow down her bowels and that she'll be able to eat again soon.

Love you all!

Later...

Amy is really groggy from surgery, asking me, did I find her wedding ring? Was I sure not to lose her earring? Does my family know I'm OK? And so on. She still hasn't opened her eyes, though. She says she feels like a truck hit her (which is normal). She just needs to sleep off the rest of the anesthesia, and I think she'll be fine.

The doctor says he's keeping her in the hospital another night because of her collapsed lung. She won't be happy to hear that when she's fully awake—she had planned to go into work tomorrow. (Insert a Mikey eye-roll here.) But the doctor says it's important to make sure her lung rebounds from having all that fluid pressing against it, crumpling it into a small ball. The doctor also says he doesn't think the anesthesia will hamper her bowel and that she can try more fluids later today. So that's good news! And the chemotherapy port is also in place—very good news indeed!

Our girl will probably be in some pain when she wakes up, so pray that the nurses help her manage that well. And even in her sleep she seems to be struggling with that smashed lung, so pray about that too please. Otherwise, things are going the way they are supposed to go—thank you, Jesus!

Thanks for sticking with us through thick and thin and lumpy lungs and all!

Thursday, May 12, 2016

Amy is home! Yay! She's going to take a nap, and then I'll make her post an update here. Here's the short story: Liquid diet for two more weeks, rest, pain management—oh, and (of course) she made the doctor write her a note so she can go to work tomorrow.

Later…

So…

Ahem…

I just got a Facebook message from James Taylor's assistant.

(I know, I'm trying to play it cool, but I'm kind of doing a little happy dance in my head right now.)

She's not making any promises, but she said she'd talk to JT when he gets back from his Canada tour in June. (!)

She also asked if we'd stop flooding James's Facebook page with my picture—so, you know, maybe we should do that.

Meanwhile, did I mention I JUST GOT A MESSAGE FROM JAMES TAYLOR'S ASSISTANT? What a crazy internet age we live in.

You guys are so cool.

Maybe this little dream will come true! We'll have to wait and see—and I'll be sure to keep you updated. Thank you so much for loving Amy enough to pester a big-time celebrity on her behalf! We love you and are so thankful to God for you!

Later…

(From Amy!)

Hello, my friends! I am home and thankful to get to nap in my own bed today! I was happy to find a Mickey care package sent from Dallas and a Mickey lantern on my porch—a great welcome home!

Thank you so much for all your prayers while I was in the hospital. I had several of my favorite nurses and CNAs and made a few new friends as well. One of the nurses even gave me flowers this morning before I left!

I am LOVING seeing all the James Taylor posts! That is so fun! Seeing JT really is the last thing on my bucket list, and I love that Mike got this started. It will be fun to see what happens—thanks to all of you for joining in the fun! You guys are great!

Keep shining, my friends!

Friday, May 13, 2016

Hi, all,

I got another note from James Taylor's assistant. She promised to ask James about Amy when he returns from Canada and asked that we stop posting our request on James's Facebook page.

Will you let your friends know to stop posting on James's page? Thanks.

And thanks SO MUCH for helping us get their attention! You guys rock!

Friday, May 20, 2016

(From Amy!)

Hi, everyone! Just a short update. I am doing pretty well—just wear out easily, so I'm moving slowly. But I AM MOVING, which is important!

I do have the tube in my side. The home-health nurse comes weekly now to drain the fluid from around my lung. Even with that, my right lung is not expanding as it should, but the hope is that after I have more chemo, the lung will be less "sticky" and will expand.

Chemo is next Thursday afternoon. Keep praying me along to get to that next point! Thank you so much—I can't do this without you all!

Monday, May 23, 2016

I was talking about you with a friend yesterday, and he marveled at your tenacity of care and encouragement.

"Usually," he said, "there's a flurry of concern at the beginning, but then that wanes as an illness drags on. In all my years, I've never seen so many people so determined to care for someone this much later. Amy's friends are very special people."

Well, yeah.

OK, you stubbornly faithful people, here are a few updates:

1. Amy is still on a liquid diet, still fighting with pain management, and determined to make it to the next chemotherapy. She's weak. She needs plenty of rest and extra sleep just to tackle the next day, so when she's not at work, most of her time is spent resting on a couch watching the rest of us play or heading off to bed. But she's in good spirits and able to work, which helps.

2. Our girl is a bionic woman now, with an infusion port in place just below her skin, under her collarbone, and a plastic tube inserted into the lining of her lung. The port will make it much easier to handle chemotherapy, blood draws, and the like. The tube sticking out just below her ribs means that when a nurse drains off excess fluid created by the cancer, she can do it here at home instead of requiring Amy to go to the hospital. They are doing drainings every five days. Yes, by some remarkable coincidence, I always seem to have some errand or chore that takes me away at precisely when it's time to suck that icky brown liquid out of her chest.

3. Eww! (Insert an image of me shuddering here.)

4. If you hug our bionic girl, please do it gently, as all those tubes and ports make her feel very tender inside.

5. **Today we go to Denver to meet with a new doctor.** We are very happy with our current team of doctors, but given the gravity of the situation, we decided a third opinion might be worthwhile. (OK, I'm the one who insisted on the third opinion. Not sure exactly what I'm expecting, but it seemed like a good idea, and our current doctor was very supportive when I asked for it.) Amy is a little nervous about seeing this new doctor, and we all hate Denver traffic, so feel free to pray that our trip today is productive and easy.

6. **No, I'm not writing anything of significance right now.** (Several of you have asked, so I figured I should just fess up.) Yes, I'm still supposed to be writing a novel, but my publisher has been very gracious and emptied my calendar of deadlines for the time being. I just can't concentrate on something that requires so much time and constant attention as a novel does. (In fact, I'm just not doing any work at all this week because I want to focus on all the things we've got going with Amy's care.) I'll pick it back up in the future when I can isolate myself for a while and immerse myself back into the fictional world where my characters live.

7. **Wednesday Amy goes in for blood tests that are supposed to tell us whether this new chemotherapy drug is working.** It'll be a few days after that before we'll get any results, but we'll keep you updated.

8. **Chemotherapy infusion #2 is scheduled for Thursday, so be sure to lay out your Mickey Mouse apparel and dust off your other Mickey stuff as a reminder to pray for her that day.** You've spoiled us by now, so we expect to see lots of Mickey pics to encourage us through the day on Thursday.

I think that's it! We love you!

Later...

(From Amy!)

Hey! Denver doctors agree with the current plan of the Loveland doctor, so that's good. They also had some ideas of clinical trials for down the road that we can look into. We're thankful to have the ability to get new insights! Thank you for praying!

P.S. Traffic was great!

Wednesday, May 25, 2016

(From Amy!)

I just got a personal video message from JAMES TAYLOR!

Later...

#JT = good medicine! HE DID IT!

James Taylor sent our girl a personal get-well video message. Cue the JT video![2]

Later...

(From Amy!)

So I got a personal video message from my new best friend JAMES TAYLOR! He chatted for a couple minutes from his studio, sharing encouragement and kind words. Super fun! I got a little teary watching it. Thank you to everyone who posted and reposted to get the message to him! What a delight!

---

2. To view the video for yourself, visit AmyNappa.com. It's pretty cool!

Thursday, May 26, 2016

(From Amy!)

While I was at chemo today, a group of beautiful elves sneaked into my backyard and transformed it into a beautiful garden overflowing with flowers! There are two vivid red recliner chairs and a little table too. And gift cards for food we can eat out there! Just overwhelmed with feelings of being loved and cared for. I keep saying "WOW!" over and over again because I just don't know what else to say! THANK YOU!

Wednesday, June 1, 2016

(From Amy!)

Tonight a large group of dear friends gathered in my honor. As I saw the faces of so many people I love, my heart was simply overwhelmed. "Thank you" never seems like enough. You all make my life so much better. Thank you for being on this journey with me and for cheering me on when I think I can't keep up. God shows me his love through each of you!

Sunday, June 5, 2016

OK, this is pretty much a shot in the dark, but…does anyone happen to have a small wheelchair we could borrow?

Before we realized that Amy would have to go through chemotherapy again, I made plans to take my girl to Denver Comic Con. Now that she's in chemotherapy, she's not really strong enough to walk around a big event like this. I asked about getting a wheelchair at the convention center, only to find out that "the Business Center at the Colorado Convention Center no longer has scooters and wheelchairs for rent. Currently there are no other onsite rentals services."

So I figured I'd at least ask you all…Thanks!

Monday, June 13, 2016

(From Amy!)

Hello, everyone!

I haven't really posted much lately on how my health is doing, and several have asked…so here goes!

I had blood work done on May 26, and they shared with me that my CA125 (the marker they test to see how the chemo is working) had gone up. This is the marker we want to be under 34. When I first found out I had cancer, it was at 3,400. When I finished chemo in January, it was at 21. When I found out the cancer was back in April, it was around 700. In May it was back up to 3,500. Not good. The doctors told me not to worry—I am still early in this new chemo, and they expect the number to go down after chemo #3. But the doctor that I saw in Denver was bothered by this number. She consulted with the doctors here, and they have decided to put me on an additional drug.

This new drug is the one that Kaiser declined to pay for last year and that the doctors hoped I would start later this year if I could get approved. They have decided to put me on it sooner, and I did get approved and have the medicine at my house. It's my understanding that I'll start taking it after chemo on June 16. This is a pill—I will take 16 pills a day (that is not a typo!), and these specifically target the cells that carry the genetic mutation that causes my cancer. I'm thankful to be able to start taking this—but could you all pray about the side effects? They don't sound like they're any fun.

I am still draining the fluid from the area around my lungs every five days. My mom and I have learned how to do this at home, using the tube that was placed in my side last month. The hope was that every time I drained it, there would be a little less fluid. But every time I drain, there is a little more fluid. So the cancer is still going strong there, and for me this means a good amount of coughing and shortness of breath. Again, there is the hope that after chemo #3 it will start to decline.

I am on a mostly liquid diet of protein shakes, smoothies, and that sort of thing. I can eat a few soft foods, such as mac and cheese, mashed potatoes, and lumpy soups. Once more, hoping that after chemo #3 I'll be able to add more to that.

The good news? I'm still working, I have been able to hug people lots, and I have had several family members come to visit recently. They have brought a lot of joy with them. Mike and I continue to feel your love expressed to us in many, many ways, and we have no doubt that God is with us through this all! Despite the challenges that the cancer brings, I still have joy every day!

Thanks for continuing to pray! I have chemo on Thursday afternoon, so break out your Mickey stuff and remember to pray for me! Love to you all!

Thursday, June 16, 2016

(From Amy!)

Hello, everyone,

I know a lot of you have been wondering what I found out at the doctor's office today. The news was not good. My CA125 has continued to rise, so the chemo is not working. They decided it was not worth having me do chemo this afternoon since it is clearly not working—no point in putting my body through that if it won't help.

I am now going to be trying two different pills. I mentioned one before. It targets the cells with the genetic mutation—that's the one I'll take 16 a day. I take eight pills in the morning and eight at night. I took eight about an hour ago—not too hard to get down…at least for the first time! The other drug is a kind of oral chemo that I hope to pick up at the pharmacy tomorrow and start taking. The doctor said the goal with these is to slow down the cancer and buy me some time.

Which leads to the hard part.

The doctor is not expecting that I am going to get better or go into remission. At this point, she said we are trying to slow things down and buy time. She was unable to say how much time. Part of it will depend on whether I respond to these new drugs. If I do, that will help. If I don't, it sounds like things will go downhill quickly.

So. It's been a weepy day around here.

Right now you can pray for peace for all of us and for these drugs to work and slow down the cancer. And pray that I will be able to keep shining the love of Jesus no matter what! I have an amazing eternal hope—but I'll be honest and say I feel sad right now. So feel free to cry, but also feel free to keep praying. I love you all, and your support is like a blanket that warms my heart!

Sunday, June 19, 2016

Two things this morning:

1. There are some wonderful people at our church. Thank you all for your kindness, hugs, and prayers over me this morning. It was health and healing for me to be there and worship.

2. When I came home from church, I found Amy suffering on the couch. She felt ill and weak while I was gone but didn't text me because she didn't want me to miss church. (Sigh.) This will surprise no one, but she quit taking some of her medications (for nausea and pain) because she thought she felt fine and didn't need them anymore. Now she's feeling the results (nausea and pain), so we have to try to get ahead of it again. Please pray that physical peace will fill her body and that she'll be able to eat without any problems. Our girl needs her strength.

We love you all!

Monday, June 20, 2016

(From Amy!)

Ever since the Green family created "That Dragon, Cancer" to honor their son Joel, I have thought of cancer as a dragon. I see it circling, flicking flames, and cruelly breathing its heat onto me, never relenting. And I see myself as the storybook maiden or princess who is standing in the path of the dragon, forced to face him down. In this picture I am never alone. I am always held up by a crowd of people who are encouraging me, holding me up, wiping my tears, and doing all they can to give me strength to keep facing that dragon.

Last Friday, Heidi P. stopped by and prayed for me. She didn't pray anything about a dragon at all, but while she was praying that same picture came to my mind. But this time there was a new figure added in. There was a knight. I did not see his face, but to me it was Jesus. He was bigger than me. That figure was standing in front of me with one hand on me and the other hand holding a sword up to the dragon.

I didn't feel like God was saying that I would be healed—but I did feel like Jesus was fighting for me.

That's all.

Later…

Hi, loved ones. Here are a few updates:

1. Amy is feeling much better today. Thank you for your prayers and support yesterday! She felt very loved.

2. This week marks the beginning of Amy having to cut back to part-time on her work hours. You know how that makes her feel, so when you and Jesus are hanging out this week, if you think of it, please pray for her emotional heart as well as her physical needs.

3. A big THANK YOU to Lily (and Jeanne) for remembering me with a fun gift on Father's Day! And a yummy THANK YOU to Genevieve (and Mandi) for also remembering me with sweet treats!

4. Amy had to miss out on Denver Comic Con after all. Oh well, things are the way they are. But I was able to go and spend some brainless time away from my troubles, being a nerd and meeting my comic book heroes. It was a welcome break, but I did miss my girl. Now it's back to real life—but it was a fun weekend!

5. Amy has been taking the oral chemotherapy for three full days now. So far, side effects have been mild. We are grateful! Thank you, Jesus!

6. It's been only four days since we found out the very bad news about Amy's prognosis, and we are facing a mountain of tasks to be accomplished—plus trying to work through our own whirlwind of emotions. We are also trying to make sure everyone who wants to spend time with Amy is able to, but coordinating schedules and managing Amy's condition and trying to help those who are grieving is just becoming overwhelming. I know I've already frustrated and disappointed many of you in this regard. Please accept my apologies, and thank you for being patient with me as we all walk down this difficult road together.

7. We have an appointment next month to learn more about how hospice works, end-of-life options, what happens when a person dies from cancer, and all those hard issues you confront in this kind of situation. But my girl and I were talking yesterday, and we were reminded that Amy is not defined by her death; she is defined by her life—and that includes today and tomorrow and however many days she has after that. We are grateful for each one.

We love you!

Sunday, June 26, 2016

(From Amy!)

Hello, friends!

This weekend was a delight, as my brother and sister who live in Arizona came to visit. It was the first time all five of us kids were together in about three years! I so love my family!

While we were together, we spent some time talking through a matter that I would like to invite you to join us in praying about.

As many of you know, our youngest sister, Annette, is developmentally disabled and has lived with Mike and me for the past 16 years. As we are facing the realities of the future, we realize that Annette will need a new living situation. Our family is in the process of learning what services are available to Annette and looking at options for a new home for her. We have done some research and are applying for assistance, but would you all please pray for us in this process? Annette is already struggling with the uncertainties, and we want to assure her that no matter what she will be loved and cared for. Please pray for her heart to be free from worry.

And if you know of services we should explore, or host families we might interview, or things like that, please private message either me or my sister Jody Brolsma. We so appreciate you joining with us in this. It's difficult to think about the changes ahead, but we do want Annette to be comfortable and to know how dearly she is loved no matter what!

Thank you for your continued prayers and for walking alongside us!

Saturday, July 2, 2016

Someday soon we'll give you all a "real" update with medical terminology and everything, but for now I'm just going to tell you a story about our three-year-old granddaughter. Last night she came over to hang out and color with Amy for a bit. When it was time for her to leave, she leaned over and patted Amy on the arm. "I think you're going to be fine," she said.

Ah, the faith of a child, right? (Cue the chorus: Awwww!)

Sunday, July 3, 2016

That's our girl in the white hat. The rest are just a small portion of about 150 people who gathered around us and showered us with love and beautiful prayers at church this morning. What a blessing! We love you!

Saturday, July 9, 2016

Hi, loved ones,

Yesterday Amy and I watched our wedding video. I have to say that my best man, Kevin Heard, had the coolest hair of all time. I was taller then, more muscular, and almost pulled off that pompadour-style thing on my head. Amy was stunning (as usual). For those of you who know her now and are curious, Amy's sister Jody was an adorable, sweet-sixteen bridesmaid, even if she was more interested in some high school dude who attended the wedding than in the wedding itself. Ah well, the show must go on, right? Hard to believe it's been almost 30 years since that day. (By the way, we had wedding pie instead of cake. It was awesome.)

Anyway, here's what's going on today…

We are in a kind of limbo, waiting to see if the oral chemo medicines will have the desired effect. Our girl is sleeping more and more, about 12 hours a night, slowing down as the days get longer. She's still working (surprised?) but maxes out at about four hours a day, after which she comes home exhausted and takes a nap. A steady stream of friends and family have been making their way to Nappaland. Just to visit. Just in case. Amy loves receiving them all. She and I have also had a few precious private moments, saying the things that need to be said. Just in case. She is both sad and joyful at the same time, something that makes no sense but is nonetheless. We laugh frequently, cry easily, and are often comforted by God's presence. And we continue to wait.

On Thursday next week, we get test results from new blood work. Those results will tell us one of two things: (1) The oral chemo is working and buying us more time with our girl, or (2) the oral chemo is not working and, well, our time may be running out. We've decided just to wait it out, to see what God will do. Does he have a third option, as yet unseen, preparing to show itself in our myopic view? We'll find out soon, I think. Whatever Christ does, it is and will be good. He is always good.

We'll let you know what we find out next Thursday.

Meanwhile, if you think of us while you're talking things out with Jesus this week, tell him thanks for always being near. We love you!

"Now we see things imperfectly, like puzzling reflections in a mirror, but then we will see everything with perfect clarity. All that I know now is partial and incomplete, but then I will know everything completely, just as God now knows me completely" (1 Corinthians 13:12 NLT).

Thursday, July 14, 2016

Well, the news is not what we were hoping, but not unexpected either.

The cancer continues unabated, and the cancer marker in Amy's blood is over 7,700. (Remember, normal is under 35, and last month she was at 4,500.) The hard truth is that there's nothing more the doctor can do, so we must drink the cup set before us. There is no timeline at this point; our doctor just says "probably sooner rather than later," which could mean weeks or even months. God knows the timing, and we'll wait for him to share that knowledge when he feels it's appropriate. The doctor encouraged Amy to just continue to do the things that bring her joy (work, anyone?) as long as she feels like it for as long as she is able. Hospice is in our future, but not in our day today, so we will enjoy the moments as they come. Tomorrow has enough worries of its own.

Pray that our girl doesn't have to suffer too much in the coming days/weeks/months. I think she's suffered enough already.

"We are troubled on every side, yet not distressed; we are perplexed, but not in despair; persecuted, but not forsaken; cast down, but not destroyed" (2 Corinthians 4:8-9 KJV).

Friday, July 15, 2016

I have to say, I admire my 81-year-old mother.

She's been a faithful encourager to me and Amy through this whole ordeal, and tonight was no exception. "The important thing is for you and Amy to have special moments together right now," she said to me. Then she made a significant sacrifice to help make that so. I know this was not easy for her, and I admire her very much for putting my emotional well-being above her own self-interests. She's pretty cool.

And just as a side note, my mother was the first one to know when Amy and I got engaged—but not because either of us told her.

We were living in California, going to college, and had been dating for ten days. Late that tenth night I couldn't keep it inside anymore, so I popped the question. Early the next morning, a phone message was waiting for me: "Call your mother. She says it's important."

"Hi, Mom. What's up?" I said when I called. She didn't bother with pleasantries like "Hello" or "How are you doing" or anything like that.

"What's her name?" she said by way of greeting.

"Um, Amy," I said.

"And?" she said.

Busted, I thought. Out loud I said, "Um, and I asked her to marry me. Last night."

"I knew it," she said. "The Lord tells mothers their children's secrets."

So my mother was the first to find out we were engaged—even though neither Amy nor I told her!

Saturday, July 16, 2016

Amy has been unable to eat for two days now. She switched to clear liquids today but couldn't keep that down. She's on three different nausea medicines, but it's still not enough. No food intake means no nutrition, which means no strength. She's moved into the guest bedroom upstairs for the time being because it's too much of a struggle for her to walk up and down the stairs.

Yeah, we might be asking for a new round of Amysitters in the coming days/weeks.

Anyway, today we went back to an old standard for fighting nausea—binge viewing of *The Big Bang Theory* on DVD. That really helps distract her mind from the constant feeling of nausea. And it was so sweet to walk into the room today and see both Amy and her sister lying in bed, dozing next to each other while *BBT* played its laughs on the TV.

We feel like these past two days are just a temporary setback. Amy has maintained good spirits in spite of it all, and yes, we're going to call the palliative care doctor first thing Monday morning. But still, our girl's got to eat. She needs her strength.

You've been with us long enough that I think you know what that means: It's time to give your knees a good workout.

Ready…set…pray!

We love you all!

Sunday, July 17, 2016

Amy had a better day today—thanks for your prayers. She still is not eating much, but she did manage to keep down some Mickey Mouse–shaped watermelon chunks and half a ramekin of pumpkin custard. Not much, I know, but it is something, so we are grateful.

Tonight we just sat on a couch and binge-watched *New Girl* on DVD. Halfway through the second or third episode, Amy turned to me and said, "This feels like just a normal night, like I'm going to wake up tomorrow and find out the cancer was all just a bad dream."

Even in the harshest hours, there are still moments like this, moments of joy and normalcy. No, this is not exactly the life we would have chosen for ourselves, but it's still a good life, filled with love and meaning. We are reminded of that in many ways every day.

Pray that our girl gets more of those "normal" moments and fewer of the harsh ones. Pray that Amy doesn't have to suffer.

Thank you!

Tuesday, July 19, 2016

Today turned out to be Amy's last day at her job. She finally admitted that she can't keep up anymore, won't ever be able to keep up anymore, so she made the phone call herself tonight.

Amy is heartbroken at having to leave her work. She's just sobbing on the couch in our family room. She knows she will never return. My heart aches for her.

I am helpless. As usual.

Saturday, July 23, 2016

(From Amy!)

Hello, friends! Thought I'd share a short update. I am now on medical leave from Group. Super hard to let go of that—you all know that being able to work has been very important to me. But my need for rest continues to grow. Plus, managing pain and nausea makes working a challenge. I'm sleeping about 14 hours a day!

A bit of good news is that I have kept food down for a few days—yay! Thank you all for praying me through these past days.

Please continue to pray—so thankful for each of you and the joy you add to our lives!

6

Fullness of Joy

In your presence there is fullness of joy;
at your right hand are pleasures forevermore.

PSALM 16:11 ESV

Thursday, July 28, 2016

Somebody asked me recently why I'm not angry at God.

I had to think about that for a moment because honestly, it never occurred to me to be angry at him. I understand that this is an awful situation. My wife is not only dying but also suffering. And all I can do is stand by helplessly while the suffering takes its toll, knowing (as we all do) where this road ends. What I don't understand is why that should make me angry at God.

In the first place, anger toward God is beyond futile. My anger changes nothing about him or me or my circumstances. Why bother with self-destructive behavior if it doesn't bring hope or healing or even some measure of relief? That just seems stupid.

But really, the answer to the original question is another question: Why would I lash out in anger toward the only thing that brings me solace? That'd be akin to punching the lifeguard who's trying to save me from drowning.

In this awful situation, I'm not warmed by anger or comforted by bitterness. Only Christ's Holy Spirit brings me peace, walks beside me in sorrow, and gives me hope not just for tomorrow but also for today—for the next hour, for the next ten minutes. Christ's constant presence gives Amy and me moments of unexpected joy, of laughter, of kinship and determination. Why would I ever push that away in exchange for a futile blame game toward the One who carries and comforts me when I feel like I can't walk another step or stop crying long enough to see the sunshine?

I must cling to Christ—desperately, determinedly, gratefully—for strength to see myself through every moment, both good and hurtful, both joyful and sorrowful. And so that's what I do. I've found Jesus to be more than sufficient. He is a man of sorrows who knows how to share mine and who tells me gently, in ways that I can believe, that in the end, everything is going to be OK. God is good; he is always good.

All right, enough of that. I actually have a reason to post today, an update to share with those we love and those who love us more than we can ever love back.

Today Amy enrolled in hospice care. This is obviously an acknowledgment that we think time is running out, but don't let this new development discourage you too much. We don't expect Amy to pass away in the next week or anything; we just want our girl to be able to benefit from all the help and services hospice care offers. In fact, they tell us Amy can stay in hospice for up to six months, and if God keeps her with us beyond that, she can unenroll or reenroll depending on her condition at that time.

What hospice really means is that Amy's doctors are no longer going to try to cure cancer. Instead they're going to focus solely on making our girl comfortable, easing her suffering, and making however much time she has left the best time possible. We are grateful for their help.

And we're grateful for you, those who have stood beside us for so long, who refuse to get tired of caring for us, praying for us, and encouraging us. We'll keep you updated. We love you!

Wednesday, August 3, 2016

Our girl is suffering today. We welcome your prayers.

Amy has been able to sleep for the past two hours and seems to be resting OK now. The hospice doctor said to give her the "heavy duty" drugs, and that seemed to make a difference. She's still not able to eat, but we are grateful for the momentary peace right now. Thank you for your prayers!

Friday, August 5, 2016

Hello, loved ones!

Many of you have asked about times to come by and visit Amy, and I've been trying to coordinate local visitors with out-of-towners. Finally, Amy and I talked about it, and we decided to make it easy for locals to drop by.

Beginning on Monday, we're going to have open visiting hours on Mondays, Wednesdays, and Fridays from noon until 12:30 p.m.

So if you want to just drop by for a short visit with Amy, feel free to come during those times. Just remember that if she's not feeling well that day, I may have to turn you away at the door—but hopefully she'll be feeling fine. We are going to block out that time and not schedule anything else then so you can be sure to see Amy as often as you like.

If you're out of town or just want longer time with Amy, I will make those visits happen too—just message me. But hopefully these new visiting hours will make it easy for those of you who are local to come by and brighten up our girl's day.

Love you!

Wednesday, August 10, 2016

Sorry to say that visiting hours are canceled today. Sorry!

Headed to the hospital...

They are making our girl comfortable. She is trying to rest. It's been a hard day for her so far. Hopefully the night will pass peacefully.

Later…

All right, thanks for your patience. Here's an update on what's going on with Amy today…

Our girl woke around 4:00 a.m. with significant abdominal pain ("Feels like there's a hole in my stomach") and relentless vomiting. Those conditions continued throughout the day today. (Seriously, how does an empty stomach of a tiny little woman who hasn't eaten for days have that much to spew out? But I digress…)

We tried the first defense of medicines, but it wasn't enough. Then we called the hospice nurse, who gave us more medicines to try. That didn't work, so we called the hospice nurse again and, well, just repeat that sequence a few times and you'll figure out what our day was like.

Finally, late in the afternoon, the nurse came to our house and asked Amy if she'd be willing to go to the hospice rooms at the hospital, where they could start medicating her through an IV. By that point she was ready to try anything, so off we went.

The hospice nurses at the hospital hooked up a pain pump that delivers continuous dosing. It also has a button Amy can push every 15 minutes or so if she feels she needs a new burst of pain medicine. That has helped with pain management quite a bit. When I left the hospital, though, she was still throwing up regularly. They were still talking about what to do to try to get that under control.

So as you can guess, it's been a trying day. It's difficult to watch our girl suffer like this. What's amazing is that she is genuinely caring and kind to others even during the worst of her moments. I think, were it me, I'd be inventing new curse words and trying to throw up on the nurse's new shoes or something. But Amy remains who she always is, which I guess is why so many people love her more than they love me.

Anyway, the goal is for the hospice staff at the hospital to help her stabilize and then for her to come home. She is very weak.

All right, I think that catches everybody up on the current situation. You know what to do.

We love you!

Thursday, August 11, 2016

The body is such a frail thing. I think sometimes I forget that, especially when it comes to Amy. She is such a strong person. Her spirit seems to expand her size and give the impression that she is larger and more substantial than she really is.

Watching my 100-pound gal sleep in that hospital bed today, I keep absently thinking the same thought: *She's so small*…

Our girl is resting quietly now. They've hooked her up to three (count 'em, three!) IVs. One is for pain, one is some sort of powerful nausea-prevention cocktail, and one is for hydration. The result of all those powerful drugs is that she can't keep her eyes open. Our son came to visit, and she slept the whole time. Thankfully, our son is the patient, understanding type. (Yeah, he got those qualities from her, not from me!)

I find myself watching her right shoulder. As she sleeps, it raises slightly every time she takes a new breath. It's kind of comforting to watch it dance its little rhythm—up, up, then a gentle slide down, down. A few minutes ago, I checked the dance, and it was in-between movements. There was a constricted moment of uncertainty on my part; I felt my own breathing stop while I waited to see what would happen next, to see if anything would happen next. And then, up, up, gentle slide down. I hadn't realized how tense my neck and shoulders were until they relaxed at the sight of her breathing.

It is such a frail thing, this temporary physicality.

Our girl is still here, stronger than she ought to be, larger than she really is. They are saying she'll be here a few days and then will be able to come back to our house. They seem to believe these hospital days are not yet her last, so we are grateful.

Last time she was awake, she told the chaplain and the nurses that she feels very loved and cared for by all of you. We both do. Please pray that our girl's suffering will subside. We love you all.

Saturday, August 13, 2016

To celebrate Amy's sixteenth anniversary at Group Publishing, her coworkers created this video.

We couldn't stop smiling as we watched it in the hospital![1]

Later...

I think, first, I need to clear up a misconception. Some of you are under the impression that I write these little updates to be inspiring, or meaningful, or whatever. I just want to be clear about that—I'm not. I don't even like this chore. Honestly, I wouldn't do it if I had a choice. But back at the beginning, my girl was overwhelmed with trying to update her family and close friends with what was going on, so I just said, "I'll take care of it." That was supposed to mean just a secret little Facebook group of 20 or 25 people. I didn't realize exactly how many family and friends Amy had. (Understatement of the year.)

Of course, now I keep updating you all because I'm addicted to your prayers and kindness and love. I find I need you. Who knew? But let's be clear—I'm

---

1. You can see this happy little video for yourself at AmyNappa.com.

not doing what you may think I'm doing. I told Amy when I started this, "I'm just going to tell the truth. That's all." And that's it. There is no other thing going on here. I don't want there to be any other thing going on.

So here's the truth: I don't want to write an update tonight. I feel like I don't have the courage or the strength.

Today was difficult. She's getting weaker.

The enormous amounts of medicines she's on make her brain synapses sluggish, and she hates that. She struggles to keep up in conversations. It's hard for her to stay awake more than a few minutes at a time. She sometimes feels inexplicably frustrated. She doesn't know why, and that upsets her even more. Her mind instinctively knows she should be thinking faster, better, longer, and she strains at her newfound limitations, both physical and mental.

She cries sometimes. I do too. More than she does, simply because I'm awake more than she is.

She hasn't been able to eat or drink anything since Tuesday. It all comes back up before too long. Another bowel obstruction, of course. Tonight she held my hand and said, "I know this is part of it, getting weaker. I'm not afraid. I just don't like it."

The hospice staff are trying hard to get her stable enough to come back home to her own bed, her own DVDs of *The Big Bang Theory*, to all her Mickeys and Amysitters and Loveland Coffee delights. They originally said they thought she'd be able to come home by Monday, with maybe one IV pump for nausea. Now they're saying it may be longer, maybe with two pumps, one for nausea, one for pain. It is a chore to keep her hydrated, which is a third problem that throws a wrench into all our best-laid plans. And we know that when she comes home, it's not because she's getting better but because she won't get better and she wants to die in her own bed.

No one can tell me how much longer she has to suffer. They all shrug and say things like, "When this happens, it could always be the last time, or it could be just a blip on a longer road." I know they're doing the best that they can, but that kind of uncertainty is a constant aggravation to me. I'm a deadline-oriented person, after all. I work better with charts and schedules and calendars set in stone. I've never been good at just waiting for "the fullness of time."

I am so weak. Several times a day I find I can do nothing but collapse into the strength of Jesus. He must carry this load; he is carrying both this load and me. I have no strength to carry myself through this. I feel both dead in my soul and alive in his Spirit, which is strange, but OK somehow. Like Amy, I'm not afraid of what's to come. I just don't like it.

Tonight Amy said she heard music. She asked if I heard it too. I had to say no. Was there really music playing somewhere? Was she caught in that groggy moment between wakefulness and dreaming? Was an angel leaking out a little bit of heaven? I don't know. I think I don't have to know.

She's getting weaker. Today was very hard.

When you speak to Jesus, tell him thank you for his constant kindness, for never taking a moment away from my need. Ask him to ease Amy's suffering with his nearness. Thank you.

Monday, August 15, 2016

Exhausted. Will have to give the full update tomorrow. Meanwhile, I promised my girl I would give you these messages from her tonight:

1. "I love you all so much! Thank you!"

2. "I'm no longer able to use my cell phone, so don't text or call me there. If you need to get a message to me, send it to Mike."

Tuesday, August 16, 2016

Yesterday morning I walked into the nurses' station and sat down. "I want you to turn off Amy's pain medicine," I said. "I want you to shut off her morphine for four hours or so."

The nurse gave me a look that said, "Why in the name of Putz and Paddy would you want to do that?" and then promptly told me all the reasons why that was a very, very bad idea. Mostly it boiled down to "Not only is that unwise medically, it's cruel to subject your wife to the excruciating pain she will have to endure without the pain medicine." Plus, there was that whole "make me comfortable" last-wishes legal paperwork Amy had filled out back in October.

Still, I'm pretty good at being stubborn. I said, "I understand. I want you to do it anyway. I need to talk to Amy, the real Amy, not the one whose mind is foggy and confused from all the morphine in her system. I need her to help me make some decisions, I need her to be able to make some hard choices and know that she made them, not me."

Next came the lecture about Amy's condition, and how, even without the morphine, Amy would probably still be confused and foggy, and she'd also have to contend with (did I mention?) excruciating pain.

I wanted to say, "Lady, ask my son about this. Once I make a decision, do I ever change my mind?" But instead I just said, "I understand that's a possibility, and if it is, I'm prepared to move forward and make decisions on my own. But I need to give Amy a chance. She's earned that from me." Finally the nurse agreed to call the doctor and talk to him.

Just a little earlier, I had sat on Amy's bed and tried to communicate with her as best I could. (I made her sister Jody stay in the room with me so there'd be a witness that I wasn't just being capriciously cruel to my wife.) "Amy," I said, "I need to talk through some hard decisions with you, OK?"

"OK."

"But I need you to be thinking clearly so you can help me figure out what to do, OK?"

"OK."

"That means I have to turn off your pain medicine. You will suffer. You remember how bad that pain was in your abdomen?"

"Yes."

"You'll feel that again while the morphine pump is off. Do you want me to do that so you can think more clearly and we can talk?"

"Yes."

"Are you sure?"

"Yes."

"OK."

She's a tough lady, our tiny little 100-pound girl.

Before long, I got another lecture from the doctor. Same song, second verse. Shut it down, I said. To their credit, in the end, both the doctor and the nurse said, "We don't agree with what you're doing, but our goal is to follow your wishes, so…" And they shut it down. The nurse insisted on leaving a push-button "rescue" active as an act of mercy in case Amy needed an escape hatch from my stubbornness.

When the morphine first went off, our girl went into a deep sleep. Two hours later she stirred. "Who will be in this conversation?" she said, eyes still closed.

"Just you and me," I said.

"And we should do this when I feel like I'm thinking clearly?"

"Yes," I said.

"OK," she sat up in bed. "I'm ready. Let's talk now."

For the next 15 minutes, she held my hand, fought increasing pain, and did what she always has done with me. For 30 years she's been my most trusted advisor, the person whose voice centers me and gives me confidence to do what's right—what's best—even if it doesn't feel right. She was thoughtful, incisive. She asked the right questions, and in the end, she made the hard decisions for me. She made the decisions that disappointed her, that made her cry, that were only choices between "awful" and "more awful." But she at least got to make them.

And then she pushed her rescue button. And pushed it again. But we still had more details to talk through, so she refused to restart the pump until she felt like we were completely done. Finally she said to me, "OK. Go tell them to restart the morphine. Go now. Now!" She really suffered awhile then while the medical staff came in and revived her sleeping chemicals. They gave her the morphine and gave her an additional injection just to make her sleep because she was in so much pain. I felt awful for being the cause of her hurt, but in the end I knew I had to make her suffer in order to better ease her suffering. (I'm sure there's some meaningful spiritual lesson in that, but I'm too tired to figure it out.)

It was the hardest thing I've ever done, looking deeply into my girl's emerald eyes and saying, "Honey, the end is upon us. You will die very soon, probably before this week ends."

I'm sorry. And grateful. Broken and being made whole. God is good; he is always good.

Later...

OK, I'm tired of people tearing up whenever I walk into the room. We can't let that become a thing, right? And besides, anyone who has ever known Amy even for just a little bit knows she's one of the most relentlessly cheerful people on the planet. So if you'll let me, I'm just going to remember a few moments that make me smile.

1. A few years ago on a Saturday, I walked upstairs in our house. Amy was whiling the afternoon away, sitting on a chair, reading a magazine, just being lazy. "Hey," I said, "look at me. I need to test the camera on my cell phone." She turned and gave me a smile. Click. One shot was all I needed. I went back downstairs; she went back to reading. And this was that photo. I mean, seriously, right? That's just not fair. She's almost 50 years old in this pic, lazing about on a Saturday afternoon, and this is how stunning she looks?

I think, after decades together, I just got used to always having someone beautiful nearby. Sometimes I'd just sit and stare at her until she told me to get her some tea or something just so she could have a little peace and quiet. She looks nothing like this picture today but is still so beautiful that sometimes I can't take my eyes off her. Sometimes I just sit and watch her sleep, and it still makes me smile.

2. Most of you know I was unexpectedly incarcerated—I mean, hospitalized—last December for emergency surgery. Amy was in the middle of chemotherapy, and her immune system was much too weak to risk coming inside the hospital to see me. So I spent most of those days alone, just waiting to get home to my girl. On my birthday (I think it was my birthday), Amy's dad appeared in my room. "Go to the window," he said. People tend to obey Norm Wakefield, so I did as I was told. Down on the sidewalk, Amy was waiting, waving her cell phone. My phone rang, and her voice was in my ear. She couldn't come in, but she couldn't stay away either.

"I feel really good!" she told me, knowing I was worried about her. "I almost feel guilty for feeling so good." Then, just to prove the point, she danced what I can only assume was supposed to be a little Irish jig out there on the sidewalk. I can still picture that moment in my head, a little (at that time) 95-pound stick of a woman, bald, standing in the December cold, bouncing up and down, grinning from ear to ear and staring up at me two floors above. I'm smiling right now just remembering it.

3. Amy's sister Jody tells me that this morning, before I came in to the hospital, they had a spirited discussion about the classic *Mickey Mouse Club* TV show. "She told me ALL of the Mickey Mouse Club 'Days of the Week,'" Jody told me, "and today is Guest Star Day." Just in case you'd forgotten.

OK, I feel better. Hope you do too. Now stop crying when you see me. Love you!

Wednesday, August 17, 2016

The past few days, many of you have turned your attention toward me, asking how I'm doing, what I'm going to do next, if I'm eating, what I need, and so on.

You are all so kind. I figure this morning I'll just try to answer the most frequent questions, so here's the "All Mike Nappa, All the Time" update:

1. What happens when Amy passes away? I think it will look something like this. First, I'm going to lock myself in my room for about 24 hours. I just want to be alone. I want to ugly-cry until I'm so dehydrated I can't pee. I will then read a letter Amy has left for me to read at that time. I will then dry-ugly-cry (remember, I'm dehydrated at this point, right?) until all I can do is sleep for 12 to 15 hours. Then I will wash my face, put on clean clothes, walk out my front door, and let people love me.

2. What about the funeral? When should we come to Colorado? What are the details? The answer: The last thing I want to do right now is event planning, so I'm not going to do it. My best friend, Kevin Heard, has taken that responsibility for me. (Big hand for the most faithful friend I've ever had!) If you have questions about that stuff, just connect with him.

3. All right, I will tell you one thing about the funeral. We will probably wait a week or two before holding it, so if you live outside Colorado, wait to hear from Kevin before you make any travel plans.

4. Am I eating? I will reassure you with this statement: Dave and Jennifer are two of my closest friends. (Those of you who live here know what I'm talking about.) For out-of-towners, yes, I'm eating. I'm fine.

5. What about your work? Are you writing? No, not really. My new book *The Raven* comes out next month. Right now I'm supposed to be helping the promotions team at my publisher to get the word out about this book, but I've abandoned them completely. (Fortunately, they are OK with this. I know. They're weird, and I love them for it.)

6. Why did you take so long to respond to my last email/text/message? And why don't you EVER answer your phone? Let's start with the second question first: I never talk on a phone. Duh. I hate telephones. The only people who try to call me are people who don't know me. I keep a cell only because it allows me to text and access the internet. If you really need to get in touch with me, you're wasting your time if you try to call. Sorry, I know people hate that about me, but I'm OK with it.

As for sometimes being slow to respond, I really am sorry about that. I do try to get back to people quickly. If you email/text/message me and I don't get back to you in a timely way, it means one of these things: (a) Amy is awake and comfortable, so I've put aside all my screens and am just enjoying time with our girl instead. (b) Amy is awake and struggling, so I've put aside all my screens to stand helplessly by and wish I could do something to ease her pain. (c) I'm exhausted and just don't want to talk to anybody at the moment. (d) I'm just being a jerk, and I'll get over it soon.

7. Long-range plans? Sigh. Mostly I don't know. I need to write one more novel, partly because my publisher has already paid for it and mainly because Amy made me promise-promise-promise I would finish it. (She read the first 100 pages and was very annoyed with me that she couldn't finish it before she died.) After that, I guess I'll start applying for jobs and see what happens. Basically, I really don't know what God has in store for me "after Amy." I'm just going to have to wait and see what happens.

All right, I think that's enough of the "Mike Nappa Narcissistic Drone Tour." Thank you for caring about me. Sorry I'm such a wad sometimes. Love you!

Thursday, August 18, 2016

Quiet day today. Amy took a turn for the worse, so we just sat near and let her sleep the hours away.

I don't know if any of you watch that old TV show *Friends*, but if you do, then Amy is Monica—always the hostess If someone is in the room, she feels obligated to chat. (She loves chatting too, but you know what I mean.) Still, she is very weak, her body is slowly shutting down, and it's nearly impossible for her to keep her eyes open for long.

When the doctor came in to make rounds today, Amy asked her, "Is it OK if I just sleep when people come to visit me? I feel like I should be keeping the conversation going, but I'm so tired." The doctor gently explained that yes, hospital regulations do allow for dying patients to sleep whenever they want to, even if there are others in the room. She seemed relieved to hear that. (I know what you're thinking and yes, I've been telling our girl that same thing since day 1 in the hospice ward, but you know how it is. Sometimes your words have no meaning until they come out of someone else's mouth.)

So we kept it quiet and mostly uneventful today. She slept. We whispered. She'd wake up long enough to press her morphine "rescue" button and go right back to sleep. She struggled with increasing pain for several hours until finally letting me report it to the nurse, who was able to bring it back under control. She slept some more.

She talks in her sleep—did you know that? I can't make out what she's saying; it's mostly whispers. Once she came partly awake when she was doing it, so I asked her what she said.

"I was praying," she breathed to me, "about the pain."

I nodded, ashamed I'd interrupted her holy communion with my crass questioning. "We are too," I mumbled. And I was. She went back to sleep.

Amy is often confused but not delirious, and it's nothing severe. She just gets a little disoriented or mixes up her conversations. She wakes up thinking that she's somewhere else or that we're waiting on her to go somewhere ("I need to get my shoes and I'll be ready")—things like that. Which means I guess I should talk to you about greeting cards and notes and such.

I've got 30 or so unread cards you wonderful people have sent to Amy. Every day I've been trying to see if she wants to read them because she loves to read them. At home, she has two large boxes filled with the hundreds of cards you've sent her over the past year, and previously she'd often pull them out and reread stacks of them at a time. But she's so easily flustered now that it's hard for her to read more than a sentence or two without losing the meaning. She's smart enough to know her mind isn't functioning as it should, and it frustrates her. When she's felt good, she's tried again to read cards, but it has become too hard for her. I've read some of them aloud to her. She likes that, but again, she's usually going back to sleep after only one or two cards.

All that to say I have 30 or so unread cards you wonderful people have sent to Amy. I'm sorry to tell you they just won't be read this side of heaven. It's too difficult for our girl, and at this point, she doesn't deserve the frustration. I'm sorry. I know each of those cards means more than the words carefully, lovingly printed on them, but when an end comes, some things just go unfinished. Please know that she knows you love her deeply, and she is very grateful.

You may be surprised to discover there are many blessed moments in a day like this despite the circumstances. Sometimes Amy will wake up and want her sister Jill to lie in bed with her and watch *Friends* on the iPad. They hold hands while they watch until Amy falls asleep. Then Jill just keeps holding her hand for a while. Maybe she'll read a book, lying there next to Amy, maybe she'll check her cell. But Amy is very comforted with Jilly squeezed in next to her frail little body.

Amy's sister Jody also came by for a few hours today and regaled us all, even Amy, with her sex-tape stories. (No, I'm not going to explain that, so you'll just have to ask Jody about it yourself.) We were laughing so hard I felt like crying again, but the good kind of crying. Then there was a serene moment when Jody was reading a book, feet up on Amy's bed. Jill was nearby, wrapped comfortably in Amy's quilt, and our girl was sleeping peacefully between two of her sisters in the open room. There was a hint of a smile at the corners of our girl's lips. I held my breath, memorizing the scene because I think it will cheer me someday when I am a sad and lonely old man. I thanked God that this kind of family peace was part of my awful, everyday experience.

Life is good, I thought, *even when death is shuffling down the hall, looking for our door*.

God is good.

We have no way of knowing how much time Amy has left. The doctors seem to think days rather than weeks. It's OK. We're going to savor these moments instead of dreading them.

And I must admit, I do like watching my girl sleep.

Saturday, August 20, 2016

OK, my wife is appalled that I said her sister regaled us with stories about her sex tape, so I guess I'll have to explain after all. At her work, Jody and her team were brainstorming teaching activities for children's ministry when someone recalled an object lesson on purity that used cellophane tape as an example. That became jokingly called the "sex tape" lesson.

Now you can get your minds out of the gutter. (And shame on you for thinking anything other than perfection out of Jody Brolsma!)

Monday, August 22, 2016

The doctor gave me a booklet to help me gauge Amy's progression as we near the end. On the first page it says, "People die the way they live."

I saw that and thought, *Yep, that sounds about right*.

Saturday, August 27, 2016

On August 3 we passed the three-month deadline of the prognosis one of our oncologists suggested for Amy. (No one predicts a death date—doctors avoid that relentlessly—but he let it slip that if treatment didn't work, he thought about three months would be left for her.) On August 10, Amy was in such physical distress that we had to take her to the hospice care center at the hospital. By Monday, August 15, I thought we'd probably reached the end of our girl, and our hospice doctor agreed, saying he thought she probably wouldn't last to the end of the week. I told my best friend to start making funeral plans. I told Jill she should come out as soon as possible for one last visit with her sister. When Amy was awake, I had her make a couple of "good-bye" phone calls to the few remaining loved ones who'd been unable to hear her voice recently.

Then I waited.

Tuesday, August 16, I realized I wanted to be wearing a Mickey Mouse shirt when Amy died. I noticed this only because I kept wearing the same two Mickey shirts, washing them, and wearing them again. So I put on a clean Mickey shirt, went to the hospital, and waited for Amy to die. Jill called to tell Amy she'd changed her flight and was coming out on Wednesday.

"I may not be here by then," Amy told her.

We all cried a little more. As the day passed, her breathing became labored. Sometimes, while sleeping, she'd stop breathing. I'd wait. Then after a moment or two (or sometimes three), Amy would gulp in air with a rush of percussive force, air filling only her left lung because the right side is swamped with fluid in the lining. Then shallow, shallow, shallow, and another big gulp. But at least she was still breathing. We got in the habit of watching her pulse throb on the side of her neck just to gauge whether she was still alive. She was barely responsive the rest of the day.

When I went home that night, I thought she'd probably pass away before I got back to the hospital the next morning. I was glad her father was with her. I can't remember if it was exactly this night, but one night during this time, my cell phone rang around 2:00 or 3:00 in the morning. *This is it*, I thought. *They're calling to tell me she's gone*. But that wasn't it. (FYI: It was an amber alert—an estranged parent had kidnapped his or her kid. The little girl was found the next morning.)

Jill arrived on Wednesday, August 17. Amy was happy to see her. So happy, in fact, she started feeling better. By Friday, August 19, God had shown his grace once more. Hospice staff had finally tamed Amy's severest symptoms. She was resting. Her mental confusion had faded a little as her body became more adjusted to her pain medicines. Oxygen helped her breathe, and best of all, she hadn't thrown up for days. I had thought my girl was as good as dead on August 15. By August 19, the doctor was saying she had "weeks rather than days left." Long story short (right, like I'm ever going to shorten a story), yesterday we were finally able to bring Amy home from the hospice care center at the hospital. Actually, the paramedics and ambulance people brought her home, but that's just semantics, right? She slept through most of the mile-and-a-half transition, but she's very happy to be home again, even if it's only a temporary stay.

Our girl is still very, very ill. She has (literally) been asleep for the past 20 hours or so, waking up just long enough to smile, look beautiful, and ask for something to eat or drink. She will fall asleep right in the middle of a conversation if you let her. She's on bedside oxygen, pain pump, nausea pump, and various other little accommodations. She will not live forever. In fact, she may not live past next week. But right now, breath and life still course through her tiny body. She's at rest and at peace, and her love is as strong today as it was back in the days before we even knew there was anything wrong. Back when we assumed that she'd be the one who'd outlive us all.

Yeah, she's pretty great.

They thought (and I thought) it'd be a miracle if Amy lasted past August 3. The simple truth is that today is August 27, and we're already 24 days into the land of grace. God is always good. We are so grateful.

We love you!

Monday, August 29, 2016

My friend Kevin has pointed out to me that when I get sad, I stop talking, so I guess I've been a little sad of late. Rather than sit around and wallow in that, I've decided to talk a little bit today—to tell you what's been going on out here at Nappaland.

Amy's been sleeping.

All right, that about covers it.

No, seriously, since she came home on Friday, Amy's has slept about 22 hours a day, waking up just long enough to eat something, or go to the bathroom, or maybe make a quick phone call to someone who just needs to hear her voice. She tried to watch *The Big Bang Theory* on Saturday, but after she fell asleep (twice), I turned it off. The hospice folk tell me this is normal, part of the progression toward the end. (There are other signs too, but sleep seems to be Amy's biggest thing right now.) Amy is peaceful, though, almost serene. She says, "It's a good sleep. I want to sleep. It feels good." That's enough for me.

So I spend my days watching her dream and thinking up ways to try to make her life easier. Because she's so limited in what she can eat, yesterday I made a list of everything I could think of that I could make for her to eat. Then I put it all into a "Room Service Menu from Nappaland Suites for VIP Guests Only."

She seemed to enjoy that, and now she "orders off the menu" whenever she wants something to eat.

I also caught a cold. No real story there except I'm very annoyed that I caught a cold, and I'm pretty sure I got it from one of you lovely ladies who hugged me because you were crying at the sight of me. Ahem. No, don't tell me who it was. I don't want to know. Anyway, having a cold means I have to keep my distance from Amy—no more hugging or lying next to her in bed while she sleeps. Sigh. This too shall pass, I guess.

I think the real reason I've been sad lately is just that I'm in what they call the "anticipatory grieving" phase, meaning even though Amy is still here, I am grieving my future sudden loss of her, and I'm mourning all the little losses I'm experiencing with her each day. Makes sense, I guess. I've decided just to grieve as much as I want. If I'm going to get through this, I must actually go through it, grieving included. I can't let myself get emotionally stuck for years just because I'm too scared to feel a little sorrow. Grief is normal, human, and something our Man of Sorrows can help me through.

One thing I still get from Amy—frequently—is that stunning smile. She smiles at me every time she opens her eyes. "I like seeing you here when I wake up," she told me today. Smiling, of course. Kind of makes it worth waiting around for. It's a reminder that even in the worst moments, God is still good. (I may have mentioned that before.)

I'm trying to get back into my work, keep my mind busy while sitting in her room. It's good, and good for me, even if progress is soooo s-l-o-w. But I can tell it's not a foolproof plan because I'm sitting here now, trying to work, talking to you instead, and I still can't keep from thinking, *I miss my girl*.

Wednesday, August 31, 2016

She talks in her sleep. I think I told you that before.

Frequently, she sits straight up in bed, looks around like she's surprised to find herself in this room, in her home, on this planet. And then smiles sheepishly at me as she lies back down to sleep.

I ask her sometimes what she was dreaming when she sits up. Near as I can tell, she's often leading a meeting at her work ("It doesn't matter what Bible translation we use as long as kids can understand it...") or doing something in the Imagination Station at VBS. Sometimes she says she's dreaming she's taking a test and she's trying to figure out why she's taking a test because she's not in school anymore. Other times she asks me, "Where's that necklace for...?" And I say, "You already gave it to her." She says, "Good." Then she starts to pull off her wedding ring. "It's the last piece," she says. "It's for you. I don't want you to forget it." I always reassure her that I won't forget it, that I will leave it on her finger until she passes, and then, I promise, I will be sure to get it. She relaxes then—until the next day when she tries to get me to take her ring again. Today she said my name. When I went over to her, she said, "I was dreaming about you. I was dreaming that you were changing the world."

"OK," I said. "I'll get to work on that." She smiled and went back to sleep.

Yesterday our son, Tony, and our grandchildren came by and spent an hour in her room, playing with toys and talking. Today she told me she heard Tony's voice—was he here? I told her no, but he and the kids came by last night. She said she didn't remember that. Then she said suddenly, "I remember seeing Genevieve's face," which, I assume was when our granddaughter came in close to kiss her good-bye.

Our girl's been awake for very short periods of time today. Just long enough to go to the bathroom a few times, to smile weakly and explain to me (again) that she's very confused and not sure when she's dreaming and when she's awake. At one point, she woke up and sighed. "Why am I still here?" she said. "I think I can do more for God if I just go ahead and die. How do I do that?"

"I don't know, honey," I said. "Only God knows. We just have to wait and see what he does." She nodded and went back to sleep.

She's talking in her sleep now; I don't know what she's saying. But I hope an angel or two is giving her a glimpse of what's to come. I pray that one of these times soon it'll be Jesus who wakes her up instead of me.

Friday, September 2, 2016

"The Christian faith makes it possible for us to nobly accept that which cannot be changed, to meet disappointments and sorrow with an inner poise, and to absorb the most intense pain without abandoning our sense of hope, for we know, as Paul testified, in life or in death, in Spain or in Rome, 'that all things work together for good to them that love God, to them who are called according to his purpose.'"

—Reverend Martin Luther King Jr., *Strength to Love*

Saturday, September 3, 2016

Back at the hospital. Amy is resting.

Later…

I watched a pigeon die once. It was one of a pair of pigeons that used to come around my backyard several summers ago. They always came to visit together, those two. They'd sit on the back fence, one right next to the other, or fly in circles around the trees, one right next to the other, or peck in the grass at whatever birds peck at in grass, one right next to the other. Amy and I called them our little lovebirds and then didn't really think about them much after that—until one bright summer day when one of the pigeons mistook our sliding door for an open window and flew at high speed right into the thick, unforgiving glass. The sound of impact was like a baseball being hit by a wooden bat. By the time I got to the back door, the little white bird was already broken and twitching on my concrete patio.

The sun was still shining. The air was still fresh with springtime. But in that moment, there was only me and this frail little body on my back porch.

My first instinct was the same as yours. Run outside, gently pick up the bird, and place it in a shoebox filled with soft tissue paper (two-ply, of course; we use only the best in Nappaland). But it was obvious there was no point to that.

My second thought was, *I hope it can't feel pain anymore, with its neck broken like that*. And then I waited. The bird blinked at me, blinked again. I wondered where its twin was, that other little lovebird that was its constant companion. It was nowhere to be seen. Again, the little eyes blinked, and I thought, *Dying always takes too much time. Moments move slowly when the end is near*. The bird didn't seem to be pleading, or angry; the eyes were just waiting— confused, maybe, but waiting. More blinking.

And then, mercifully, it was honestly as if a light began to dim behind the eyes. I could track it like a slow-motion light wave. First the bottom part of the eye went dim, and then, like water slowly rising, the line of shadow rose halfway, then two-thirds. When it reached the top of that little bird's eyes, I knew its life had finally gone. I didn't know that bird, never even named it, yet I felt a sudden loss, like there were stories I'd never hear because I'd cleaned my patio door too well. (After that, we put stickers on the back door—just as a way of saying, "Hey, birds, and maybe children, just to let you know, there's a door here!" But that day we had no such things.)

Today, watching our girl suffer, I found myself remembering that little pigeon, thinking again, *Dying always takes too much time*. Regardless of whether there are only moments between cause of death and loss of life, or weeks, or years, the time between those two points grinds at a pace that lags behind the actual amount of time that passes. Forget the comforting lie they tell you in emergency rooms or TV shows. The real truth is that no one dies instantly. The body fights too hard and for too long for that to be true.

But I digress.

I watched a little pigeon die once. It was awful, yet held its own kind of tranquility and beauty. It was only a few moments, but it gave new texture to the life I've lived since. Likewise, for the past year or so, we've been watching a similar kind of awful beauty in every breath, every motion, every gentle flutter of Amy's beautiful emerald eyes. It is devastating. It crushes my soul in places I didn't know existed. And yet…

Amy has suffered these past few days. I have no idea if we are finally nearing the end or just going through another rough patch. I've been wrong about that a few times before. (She's such a strong, weak thing.) Regardless, today I felt like I was looking again into that little white bird's eyes, watching them blink, measuring a slow-rising shadow, wishing for mercy, feeling more than helpless.

Our girl is at rest now, comfortable and well cared for at the hospital. Please pray for Christ's Holy Spirit to envelop her with his mercy tonight. And for me too. We love you.

Later…

Sorry for my melancholy earlier. Plenty of time for that in the days to come. For now, though, let me give you the full update.

As you know, Amy was able to come home last Friday. She was very happy—and has pretty much slept through the past week, which was OK. The past few days, as she's declined physically, she's also been getting more and more confused. Beginning yesterday, she's been pretty much in a constant state of dreaming, whether awake or asleep. She understands what's going on, and it frustrates her because she can't communicate the way she is used to communicating (and, as you know, she is a very articulate person). Along with this, she's become more anxious and somewhat agitated. This is, apparently, normal. In fact, it's so normal they have a name for it—terminal agitation.

It finally got to the point where we had to have her return to the hospice center at the hospital because (without being aware of it) Amy was endangering herself, and we were having trouble keeping up with her. (You know Amy; if she wants to do something, she's pretty much going to do it sooner or later.) At the hospital they were able to give her medicines to help calm her and allow her to rest peacefully. We were dismayed at having to bring her out of her home, and yes, she cried when we told her it was time to go back, but she understood and agreed, and we are grateful that she is now able to rest. Tomorrow, as they say, is another day.

Thank you for your constant kindnesses to us. Please pray for Christ's Holy Spirit to wrap us all in his mercy tonight. We are all very tired. We love you!

Sunday, September 4, 2016

Amy is no longer able to open her eyes. She has such beautiful emerald eyes.

I will never see life in those eyes again.

I am poverty.

Later…

So I did something stupid tonight. I had to clean out some old emails to make room, and I stopped when I got to July–August 2015 and saw Amy's email address in there. Yeah, I read 'em. I'm so stupid.

My girl was in high spirits a year ago. Me too. Amy's emails are filled with delight about planning our trip to Disneyland and the D23 Expo conference. ("We have reservations for two on Thursday, August 13, at 5:30 p.m. at Rainforest Cafe. Yay!") On July 15, she sent me an email with the subject line "I'm worried…" Inside she'd written, "Not that I believe in omens or anything… but I forgot to wear earrings today! ACK!" (Yes, I brought earrings to her at her work—the fun, pink, Cinderella-shoe earrings.) And she was perpetually happy about things like going to the gym with our daughter-in-law, Mandi; going to get frozen yogurt with everybody in our family on Tuesday nights; watching *So You Think You Can Dance* when her sister Jill was visiting; and a million other random, uneventful things that brought her joy. ("I'm at Sprouts! Want me to get anything?") Best of all, every single email from her always ends with LOVE YOU! (yes, in all caps—and then she'd add a zillion exclamation points) or CAMM! or MMT! These were our secret codes for the same thing. (In case you're wondering, CAMM means "Captain America–Mickey Mouse" and MMT means "Mickey Mouse Tattoo," a reference to the matching MMTs we got during our twenty-eighth anniversary vacation).

And then there are emails about making a doctor's appointment…doctor says it's probably just constipation…lab tests…lab tests say it's just a bladder infection…need more tests…ultrasound…joking with the ultrasound tech about leaving for Disney the next day and the tech laughing and saying, "Don't worry, if it's anything really serious, I won't let you leave the office ha-ha—huh. I don't mean to scare you, but I can't let you leave the office just yet…" And then the "Well, what is it?" updates, and in between all these are emails like "Good news! I got a SHADED parking space at work today!" and "They finished painting and moving furniture in my new office!" And then an email from me telling her I was canceling the Disney trip because I couldn't take a chance that she might have some serious illness that could be exacerbated by roller coasters and airline flights, and then the first heartbreak when she wrote back to me, "Well I'm sitting here crying. I am so sad." Then two days later, on Friday, August 14, "I tried to convince [the nurse] that I am not having a medical emergency if I stay seated and relaxed, but she said there is more fluid each day, and it puts more fluid around my heart, which is not good. So…want to go to the emergency room with me?" (How's that for a hot date on a Friday night?) And finally, on August 17 she sent me details about her emergency surgery schedule, car rides, and human resources paperwork and ended with "LOVE YOU! Here we go on a new adventure."

And now, here's the secret I haven't told anyone—not my best friend, not even Amy. I've known from almost the beginning how this was going to turn out. On August 18, the day before her surgery, they were planning to honor Amy at her work to celebrate her 15-year anniversary during an all-staff meeting. She was under too much stress from all the sudden changes, too emotional, so she left work early and came home instead. Our family was coming over for dinner to spend time with Amy and have one last "normal" night before surgery-chemotherapy-recovery-whatever. All the grown-ups were eating grown-up food, but Amy wanted to make sure there'd be something our granddaughter Genevieve (then two years old) would want, so she decided to make up a batch of macaroni and cheese. I was sitting on a couch just outside the kitchen, just looking at her and being worried and grateful at the same time.

She was still in her work clothes, looking smart and sexy. She glided through the kitchen with practiced ease in a place where she felt just as comfortable as she did in the boardroom at work. Music was playing, and she was singing along. It was a peaceful place, a little calm before the storm to come. And I heard God's voice speaking unmistakably into my heart, "Memorize this moment. Keep it close to you, because right now you are looking at a living ghost."

I felt something break inside me, but it didn't make a sound. "How long?" I asked, never taking my eyes off the beauty who glanced back and smiled at me from the kitchen. There was no distinct answer, but the impression I got was a year or so—that I had only about a year left with her. I tried to tell myself it was just my fears, just me talking to myself with worry. But even though I don't hear an audible voice, God has spoken to me enough times that I've learned to recognize that voice when it rustles inside me.

So I knew. I've always known, ever since that night, what the truth was. And I saw it again in the doctor's eyes after the surgery, and I hoped I was just seeing things. But still, I knew. I just didn't know how to say that to anyone—to so many people who've been praying for that miracle, to my girl, who held out hope with her "miracle test" all the way to the end. I'm sorry. It hurts me sometimes to know something I know no one else wants to know, but I still didn't tell this secret.

So today, a little more than a year later, I spent all day just holding my girl's hand while she trembled and tossed in her sleep. She's heavily sedated now, nonresponsive mostly. Emaciated and weak, unrecognizable to most, I'd think, from the way this cancer has taken her body. But I needed to feel her touch anyway while it's still warm. I miss her touch so much.

Of course, we all know that at this point we're just waiting to see when Jesus will finally end her suffering. The nurses won't say it out loud, but it's clear to anyone with eyes. I know Amy's ready for what's to come; I just wish I was ready. People keep telling me that "it's obvious" I'm Amy's "rock" helping her through this time. What no one seems to understand is that for 30 years now, and even during this whole cancer experience, she's been my rock, the mooring I cling to, and it's so hard for me to do this without her. She sat up at one point, unable to say more than "OK" or do anything but stare straight ahead. But she squeezed my hand—held my hand in both of hers for a moment. It was too short, but it was there. "I love you," I said. Her mouth didn't move, but I heard her whisper, "I know." I think those might be the last words she'll speak to me.[2] And then she couldn't hold herself up anymore. She slumped back into the bed, dreaming again before her eyes fully closed.

So yeah, I did something stupid today—before I was ready for it, even when I knew I wasn't ready. And now I find myself praying only anguish, not even words. I just keep saying, "Jesus…Jesus…Jesus…" I know he hears me; I know he knows what I mean, knows what I need.

Jesus. Jesus. Jesus.

---

2. They were.

I don't even know what I'm supposed to ask from you now or why I wrote this enormously long post tonight when I should be sleeping, or at least trying to sleep. I guess I just needed to tell somebody how stupid I am. And you know, maybe you should remind me to drink a lot of water tomorrow, because I'm very dehydrated from crying all night tonight.

I love her so much. I know you do too. Thank you for loving my girl and for always listening.

P.S. She left some notes for you—not necessarily letters but thoughts about you in her "last things" journal. When this is finally all over, when we're all breathing again, I'll be sure to post some of those thoughts for you here. I just don't have the strength to do it now. Sorry.

P.P.S. Spoiler alert: Mostly she just says how great you all are and how much she loves you. OK, goodnight.

Monday, September 5, 2016

OK, I'm feeling better this morning. I mean, not ready to get out of bed yet, but ready to have my *Dan in Real Life* moment and face another day. Thanks for praying me through last night when I was weepy and weak and a little bit lost. Besides, you all know by now I'm pretty much a big crybaby.

Anyway, I woke up thinking I should delete last night's tear hemorrhage, but I've been informed that I'm not allowed to delete something once I post it. So sorry about that. Skip last's night's post if you don't want to be super depressed.

Meanwhile, I just wanted to tell you I'm OK. Thanks for helping me last night, and you know, in the end everything will be OK. It's just going to take a little time for us all to get there. If I want to get through this, I have to actually go through it. Sorry I keep leaving a trail of tears behind me as I go. I have plenty of happy stories to tell too, so I'll try to pull out one of those next time. Love you!

Tuesday, September 6, 2016

It is close to the end. Today the doctor told me that my sweet, sweet girl—my love, my life, my Amy—has only 24 to 48 hours left. I can't stop weeping. I am lost and broken. It feels like I will never be whole again.

I was weeping over Amy today, talking to her, just telling her I loved her, I loved her, I loved her. And I got out the ChapStick to moisten her lips. As I was doing it, I said in a shaky voice, "Honey, when you see Jesus, be sure and tell him I kept my promise. Tell him I put ChapStick on your lips all the way to the end."

The inside corners of her eyes grew dark and moist. She was so dehydrated, yet she was crying anyway, at least as much as was possible. And even though she couldn't lift her own head at this point, couldn't open her eyes even, she unleashed great effort and tried to raise her arms, to reach toward me. She couldn't make it; her arms dropped back to the bed. But I knew what she was doing.

Amy was trying to hug me. My girl was trying to comfort me one last time.

I leaned down and hugged her as gently as I could. I love her so much, and I know she loves me the same. Even here, almost all the way to the end.

Wednesday, September 7, 2016

I think it was probably a mistake because it upset her so much that it took an hour of bolus (pain) shots and some Ativan to get her calm again, but hindsight is 20/20 I guess.

Today Amy and I were alone for a while. She had been positioned onto her right side, still in a coma, with space behind her on the bed, and suddenly I felt like I couldn't breathe anymore unless I'd wrapped my arms around her frail little body one last time. So I climbed in beside her, pressed my chest against her back, and laid my head on her side, just holding her, just needing to feel her heart beating next to mine. And she knew it, she felt it, and tried to rouse herself from her drug-induced sedation. Her eyes moistened again (why do I always make my girl cry?), and she tried with great effort to roll toward me, to put her arms around me. I tried to back away and calm her, but she was inconsolable until I finally put my head under the crook of her arm, until the weight of her weakness allowed her to hold my head close to her heart. Only then did she settle in the bed. I stayed that way a few minutes, loving her warmth next to me, worried that I was hurting her for my own selfish intimacy.

And then, too soon, all the effort took its toll. She started writhing in pain, groaning, hurting. It really is best if she can just stay asleep.

Her soul is so kind that she still wants to comfort me when I am crushed beneath this moment, all these moments. I feel sad that she suffered, yet I now treasure those three minutes or so when she wrapped my head in her arm, when she was adamant, unrelenting against all obstacles to do it, even though she couldn't open her eyes, couldn't raise her head, could barely raise her arms, couldn't even roll on her back. Even though it was hurting her, she reached out to hold me as close as she possibly could.

I die again just remembering her little rabbit heartbeat in my ears.

It took me more than an hour to help ease her pain after that.

I hope it was worth it for her.

Thursday, September 8, 2016

It feels like Old Nurses Week in here today. So far, four of Amy's old nurses have come in either before or after their shifts just to sit by her bed, hold her hand, cry a little, kiss her forehead, and say good-bye. So sweet. Thank you, God, for compassionate people. (Brianna Brolsma, I hope you're paying attention.)

Later...

I am posting these here, now, so they will be public, so I will have to be accountable for them. I can't shake these lies right now, but over time I plan to cross each one off this list, one by one, until I am free of them all again. Over the next few years, you have my permission to ask me from time to time, "Crossed anything off your list lately?" Love you.

September 8, 2016

Lies I believe right now (but I refuse to believe forever)

1. I will never be truly happy again.

2. I will never be known, truly known, by anyone ever again.

3. All my best days are behind me.

4. I have failed my best girl when she needed me most.

5. I am empty, broken, and unfixable.

6. I will never be safe again.

7. I will always be afraid.

Saturday, September 10, 2016

Amy has been in a coma for six days now. She hasn't been able to eat or drink anything for seven. Doctors warned us earlier that if a healthy person (like you or me) were to go without water the way she has, that healthy person usually lives only three to five days. Doctors are always wrong, huh? They thought Amy was going to die on Thursday night. We gathered in her room to wait and watch and console each other. About four hours later, people started to go home. Now here we are two days later, and our girl, weak as she is, is still breathing. Go figure. Nurses say "she has a young, strong heart" (Gold's Gym, anyone?) that just keeps beating and a strong, strong spirit that knows how much love she is leaving behind.

We keep telling her to let go, to grab hold of Jesus's hand and move on to heaven. Yesterday, I thought about that and almost laughed. I could just see Amy rolling her eyes at me and saying, "Give me a break already! What do you think I've been trying to do? You think I like lying here in a coma waiting to die? Please." She'd been asking why she wasn't dead already for more than a month before this coma. So no, honey, I know you were ready to go from this painful place. Sorry for thinking otherwise. You do what you need to do in the time you need to do it, and we both know that one day we'll meet again in a place where pain and time are unnecessary.

It is strange that she keeps getting more beautiful as each agonizing day passes. Had she survived this last round of chemotherapy, she would have returned to being stunning—as usual. Her hair is growing back nicely, a little darker than before, thick and soft. Her eyebrows have filled in and look like they've been sculpted at a beauty parlor. Her lashes are back, thick and dark like butterfly wings. Every time a new set of nurses come in, I hear them whispering to each other "Wow, she's just so beautiful" and "I know; she is gorgeous." Her toenails are still painted in a bright, fun, pink polish. So Amy.

She doesn't dream anymore, no rapid eye movements underneath her eyelids. I think that's a blessing. She doesn't groan anymore, or shudder, or grimace. I opened her eyelids yesterday, just because I needed to see her emerald eyes again. They were stunning but empty. Two clear, blank gems, still beautiful but lacking the light that once made them shine and sparkle.

I think she is already more gone than here.

Please pray for God's mercy on our girl, for her spirit to be allowed to finish the trip that her young, strong heart keeps fighting so hard to prevent. Amy loved you all very much.

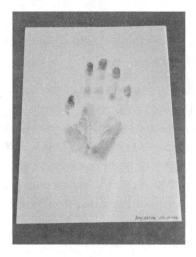

Amy's fingerprints, September 10, 2016

Sunday, September 11, 2016

Amy Nappa

November 10, 1963–September 11, 2016

Monday, September 12, 2016

Last year, Amy asked me why I didn't want to try to pull together a book from the Facebook updates about her fight with cancer. I sighed and tried not to cry as I said the obvious: "I don't want to write the last chapter of that book."

So this is not Amy's last chapter. I still don't know how to write that. But I have spent all day crying (and yes, I'm THAT dehydrated now), so before I try to sleep tonight, while my tears are momentarily dry, after all your steadfast prayers for our girl, I think you deserve to know what happened when God's mercy finally came to settle among us in Amy's hospice room.

On Thursday, September 8, the hospice team told us the end was only hours away, that Amy would be dead by 6:00 or 7:00 that night. Our family gathered around her to wait and watch and cry. Tony was there, and Mandi, Jody, Norm, and Winnie, and me. We waited, talked, took turns in the "hand-holding seat" next to her bed. We FaceTimed with Jill so she could spend a few moments crying with us. Amy never moved, but she kept breathing. By 8:00, people started to leave until finally, around 9:00, only Norm and I were left. We tried to sleep.

Every day since then we waited. Our girl never moved, but she kept breathing. Friday. Saturday. And so we waited.

On Saturday morning, September 10, I went home for about an hour. I'd seen myself in a hospital mirror and decided that I looked awful. *If this is going to be Amy's last day on earth*, I thought, *then she deserves for me to at least shave, shower, and put on a clean shirt*. So that's what I did. I shaved, showered, and put on a clean Mickey Mouse shirt for her. (It was the brown "classic" style T-shirt she bought for me when we visited Disney World for our twenty-fifth anniversary.) I even put on my only pair of blue jeans that doesn't have a hole in the knee. I thought she'd approve.

When I got back to her room, my girl was still breathing.

We spent the day listening to Group VBS songs from a mix on YouTube. I laid myself down next to her a few times, just to hold her a bit longer. I whispered sweet nothings in her ear (even though I know she always hated the way that tickles—oh well, I liked it). I held her hand and felt it get cooler and cooler. I read her favorite Scripture, Psalm 16, to her, emphasizing verse 11: "In your presence is fullness of joy."

At one point, Amy's sister Jill posted a picture on Facebook of a paragraph from Amy's 2001 book, *A Woman's Touch*. It was all about how every woman has the power to leave indelible fingerprints of love on everyone she knows. We all agreed that pretty much described Amy. I showed it to a couple of the nurses, and they loved it. Half an hour later, they were back in the room. They'd made a few calls, gone to the maternity ward, and gotten a fingerprint kit. In just the most thoughtful, kind thing ever, they made a print of Amy's hand for me, made it while my girl's hand was still warm. They gave it to me as a keepsake. They seemed happy to make me happy. (Yes, I cried.)

Around 5:00 in the evening, I finally found the courage to read to Amy a letter I'd written to her earlier in the week. There are no real secrets in the letter; it's mostly just a long thank-you note. But it was important for me to write it all down before she died, to read it to her unhearing ears. She didn't even twitch or blink, but I felt better saying a proper thank-you to my girl. She stuck with me for 30 years, after all.

Amy's dad, Norm, showed up around 6:30 in the evening. We watched about a half an hour of *America's Got Talent* (a show Amy really enjoyed), and by 8:30 I was exhausted. I'd been sleeping in a cot beside Amy's bed since Tuesday night, September 6, so I just collapsed there while Norm finished up his nightly routine and turned off the lights for us. I went right to sleep.

I woke up at 1:18 in the morning on Sunday, September 11.

No reason, really. Didn't need to go to the bathroom, wasn't uncomfortable. Just awake. I assume it was the Lord's doing. Amy told me once that she wanted me to be there when her moment of passing came, wanted me to be near. I believe maybe this waking was God's gentle way of making sure that last wish happened. An awful thing for me, yes, but also a true privilege—a singular honor to bear witness to what came next. I'm grateful I was made awake at this moment.

I got up and checked on Amy. She was still breathing. Her heart was still beating. But her body was very cool. I crawled back under my covers and tried to go back to sleep.

Ten minutes later, at 1:28, I heard Amy's voice, strong and loud in the quiet of the room. It was kind of a mixture between a hum and a moan, and it beat three times like this: "HmNnnnh. HmNnnnh. HmNnnnh." One long breath, three short hums.

Amy hasn't been able to speak for a week, I thought. *How is her voice sounding out so clearly now*? I checked the clock and then jumped up to look at her. I didn't see any breathing, but she'd fooled me dozens of times in the past week with sleep apnea that lasted up to 30 or 40 seconds. I put my ear on her frail chest to see if I could hear anything going on inside her. There was a faint heartbeat, and I thought, *False alarm again. She's still living.* Then I raised my head and continued to hear the heartbeat…it was my own, thrumming fast in my ears. I tried listening again, tried to separate the sound of my own life from hers, and registered only silence inside her chest. I looked again at the clock. Three minutes had passed since her last breath. I felt like throwing up. I held my breath and waited two more minutes.

She's gone, I said to myself at last. *I think she's gone.*

I woke up Norm. Of course I was weeping. "She hasn't taken a breath in five minutes," I said. "I think she's passed. Would you go get the nurse and ask her to check for me?" He left and was back in a moment with the two night nurses. The RN put a stethoscope on Amy's heart and listened for a good long time. Then she stood up and spoke gently to me: "She's passed."

Tears sprang fresh again, and unquenchable sorrow, and relief. The nurses left to do their duties. Norm and I wept and hugged. "Lord," I prayed aloud, "we release Amy's spirit to you. Thank you for welcoming her into your presence, into the fullness of joy." We cried some more.

The nurses returned. They gently gave Amy one last sponge bath, cleaning her well, even brushing her teeth and wiping sleep out of her eyes. They removed from her body all the offensive wires and tubes and the Foley catheter, even wiped up leftover urine. They put Amy's own pink underwear on her (which matched the pink polish on her toenails!), covered her up to her neck in a sheet, and let her body finally rest in peace. Norm and I tried to go back to sleep, to wait for sunrise. Neither of us was terribly successful.

In the morning, after Norm left, I was finally alone in the room. I went to say a last good-bye and realized there was no point. It was good for me to see Amy's body like this, I decided, here in the cold light of day. The body without the spirit really is just a casing. Just a jar of clay. This is obvious when you see it firsthand, close up. So I kissed that body's forehead but didn't bother saying another good-bye. My girl, our girl, was already long gone from that temporary thing. I found that made me smile within my tears. I didn't expect that.

Next thing I knew, the funeral home had sent a representative to collect Amy's casing and wheeled it away, covered in a thick fleece blanket.

Now I'm home, and all that's left is for me to cry some more and then wash my face, put on clean clothes, and walk out my front door so people can love me through this grief. I feel God's Holy Spirit close by me in every room of my house, and yet his spirit is unwilling to take away my pain. Instead, he is choosing to walk beside me as I suffer, much in the way, I guess, that I did for Amy. It is a hard way to live, but I think he intends to make me strong, somehow, within this great weakness. We'll see what happens.

I miss Amy so much. It feels almost like what I imagine a panic attack feels like. Maybe it is a panic attack—a relentless, hours-long, drawn-out, cruel one. I keep expecting her to come home—knowing all the while she's never coming home, not anymore. It's agonizing. I must now figure out how to live without her, and that thought terrifies me. So for tonight I'm going to focus only on the next ten minutes. I'll leave the rest, as Amy would say, as "a problem for Future Mikey."

God is good. He is always good. Tonight, when you and Jesus are talking about us, please thank him for mercifully loving Amy home today. And please ask him to mercifully love me back to safety here in the land of living too.

Thank you.

Postlude

Wednesday, September 14, 2016

I got Amy's cremated ashes from the funeral home today. (The guy kept calling them "cremains," which just seemed weird, but I digress.) They were inside a plastic bag that was in a thick plastic box. It was a cool, sunshiny, quiet afternoon, so I decided to spread my girl's remains in the peace of that moment. But I couldn't get the box open! An hour later, I finally pried apart the lid with a screwdriver. It popped open easily then. Maybe I was supposed to do that at the beginning? Rookie mistake, I guess.

I looked inside the box and wondered what I was supposed to feel. It seems surreal that the person who for 30 years filled your days and nights with life and joy and kindness, who turned your head with her sexy walk and excited your mind with her stunning insight and creativity, the woman whose smile made your heart flutter and whose nearness made you feel safe could be so easily, so quickly, reduced to a small bag of coal-colored ash.

I went outside and sprinkled the ashes of the woman who used to fill my arms (and my dreams) among the roots of two huge, 15-foot-high lilac bushes in our backyard. She loved those lilacs when they were in bloom. In spring, she'd go out every few days to gather a few fragrant flowers and put them in a bowl on our kitchen or living room table. I always liked that. So I thought our girl might like to have her remains placed there in that beautiful, peaceful spot.

I added a little marker to her resting place, a Mickey Mouse garden statue. On the statue I wrote "Amy! 1963–2016" in thick black Sharpie. Then in fine-point Sharpie I wrote, "Based on a true story," which was something she'd always joked that she wanted to have on her gravestone. (Well, honey, it's not exactly a gravestone, but at least it's there, just like you wanted. I hope it makes you smile when you see it from heaven.) In the branches above the little statue, I hung an outdoor garden ornament of Mickey and Minnie Mouse snuggling close together on a rope swing. I think Amy would have liked that too. I hope so. I said a prayer out loud, whispered into the air, thanking Jesus for giving me Amy, for the time we had before today—for all of it, even up to 1:27 a.m. this past Sunday.

And then I felt the crushing weight of her absence again. I wept, under the gentle swinging of Mickey and Minnie wrapped in each other's arms. There was a time when Amy and I would have pretended it was us hanging onto each other and that tiny, romantic rope. There was a time.

Saying good-bye again to my girl left me weak and dull. It was so hard, is still so hard. I keep wishing our good-bye was a temporary thing, like when she used to go on a business trip or I traveled to see my high school buddies. But no matter how hard I wish, my head denies my heart's desire, and so I cry fresh tears, as if I'd somehow forgotten that death is a permanent thing, as if I am surprised anew to discover my girl won't be coming home. I will go to her one day, but she'll never return to me.

Finally I went inside and listened to my "Ain't No Sunshine" playlist one more time. I know she told me not to get too lost in that mix for too long. But I think she would have understood today.

It's nighttime now, and I'm feeling a little better. I mean, I haven't cried for at least two hours, which is pretty good for me at this point. And earlier, at dusk, when I looked back into those lilac bushes through my kitchen window, I found a small smile on my lips. It didn't stay long, but it was there, so that's something.

I think (well, I hope) that smile will show itself again from time to time, through the fall and winter months when Mick and Min will huddle close to keep each other warm on their swing and into next spring when my wintry world will begin to thaw and Amy's lilacs will finally start to bloom.

Afterword

Condolences from Pete Docter[1]

October 6, 2016

Mike,

So sorry to hear of the loss of Amy. Thanks for letting me know. Hope you had great adventures together...

...and will have many more.

Pete

And now for the rest of the story...

---

1. "Carl" sketch by Pete Docter. Copyright 2016 Pixar Animation Studios. Reprinted with permission. Pete Docter is a two-time Academy Award-winning filmmaker at Pixar Animation Studios. He is the creative force behind hit movies such as *Up*, *Monster's Inc.*, and *Inside Out*. As Amy and Mike Nappa approached the end of her battle with cancer, Pete was an unexpected ally, a friend indeed—perhaps his greatest achievement of all.

During and after Amy's illness, one surprise was the encouragement I received from Pete Docter and his staff at Pixar Animation Studios. (I know, right?)

We'd met Pete during a press junket for his movie *Inside Out* just a few months before Amy was diagnosed with cancer. When he found out, Pete immediately sent a card (complete with hand-drawn sketches of his movie characters!). Amy was so thrilled to receive it that she had it framed and kept it near her bed until the day she died.

Just after Christmas that year (Amy's last Christmas), the staff at Pixar sent our girl a care package of Pixar products—books and apparel and autographs and more. Amy was delighted, of course. The following February, Pete won his second Academy Award for the fantastic film *Inside Out*. (Way to go, Pete!)

And then the end came for Amy, and Pete and his staff didn't forget the lonely old guy left behind. First there was a sympathy card signed by a large group of people at Pixar. Then a note from Pete himself, along with a hand-drawn illustration of Carl from the movie *Up*, holding a blue balloon, sympathizing with my sorrow.

Yeah, I still get teary when I look at that carefully sketched image of Carl. I think I probably always will.

As before, I am grateful.

Appendix

Letters from Amy

Sunday, May 1, 2016

(From Amy!): A Letter to Everyone

It may be the oddest thing I've ever done—walking through Target today to look for this journal, knowing I was looking for a place to write my final thoughts and memories as a way of capturing them. What do you choose when you're writing the last things? Pink? Flowers? A Bible verse? Well, this simple green book is it. And here we go.

Last August I was diagnosed with cancer. In January I had my last chemo. In February I was cancer-free. Then…on Friday I learned that my "cold" was really three liters of fluid around my right lung—most likely caused by cancer. Dang. In the next few days, I'll learn what's wrong and what's next. But since it's not looking great, I think it's time to capture a few things. Letters to my dear family. Memories someone might want to recall years from now. Maybe some silly things just in case.

Things I hope everyone remembers about me…

…My love for God. I became a Christian on Easter morning when I was four years old. I have never been a perfect Christian and have had plenty of rough spots—especially in my high school and early college years. But God has always been faithful. Always good. Always merciful.

My favorite book of the Bible is Psalms, and Psalm 16 is my favorite of those. Think of me when you read it. I have read it hundreds of times.

…My love for my family. Mike and Tony—we sure have had a great time! I'll write to you separately, but wow, I love you. My parents—loving, warm, godly. My sisters and brother, who have laughed and cried with me…and shared the backseats of station wagons…and endured camping. And my nieces and nephews who make me love life more. Mandi, Genevieve, Cayde—all joy to me. Erik, Todd, Lisa—making our family complete. I'm sure my friends always think I talk about my family too much. But I can't help myself! I love my family! This clan is my favorite group of people in the world!

My best memories are times with my family. The more laughter and storytelling and general goofiness, the better! Keep it up!

…My love for my friends. Yes—all of you. We've had great adventures over the years. And now as it seems closer to the end, you have crowded around me and loved me well, feeding me and caring for me and nurturing my soul.

Those are the most important.

Wednesday, May 4, 2016

(From Amy!): A Letter to Mikey

("May the Fourth be with you!")

I was talking to Jill on the phone tonight—telling her about the last-minute efforts to get a PICC line or Powerglide and your adamant stance that I get help. She commented that I'm lucky to have you because you always stick up for me.

I am lucky.

So I'm not being like Rachel and skipping Ross. But I also don't plan to say everything in this moment. This is a start.

I love you. No secret there. I can't really say it enough or with enough feeling or passion. It's the simple truth.

You are strong where I am weak. You are romantic when I'm not. You're adventurous when I'm afraid. You are so handsome. Creative. Smart. Kind. Generous. Funny (but not funnier than me).

Top two things about you:

1. You love God.
2. You love me.

Thank you for not skipping out on God or me when things got hard. And harder. Your faith helped me be stronger. Your love for me let me rest.

As I'm writing this, "Ain't No Sunshine" is playing on the stereo. Are you listening to that mix a lot these days? Find the time to let sunshine back in. Grief is good. So is sunshine.

Tomorrow is my first chemo. First in round two at least. I'm afraid. What if it doesn't work? I so wanted to grow old with you. I'm hoping it *does* work—so at least I can grow a little older with you.

OK, enough weepy stuff for today. Go watch something that will make you laugh. I'll share more thoughts another day.

Oh, in case you want them, we still have all the notes from the Hart Hall mailbox days. I think they're in a round box on the floor of our closet.[1] Those are the start of this story.

Friday, July 8, 2016

(From Amy!): A Letter to Tony

Today I was praying for you (I do that a lot), and you texted that you didn't get the YouTube job. Disappointment.

It's so hard as a parent to see your child—even your grown-up child—experience disappointments or challenges or setbacks. You've had your share. I appreciate your steadfastness through it all. I know life feels hard a lot of the time. Yet you keep trusting God. Keep worshipping. Keep remaining faithful to our faithful God.

I hope that when I'm gone, you'll still see God's goodness. Still see his love for you. Still find joy each day. It's been a challenge for me this past almost year to keep seeing good and finding joy. There have been days I felt like staying in bed and crying. But God keeps showing me love. Grace. Mercy. Peace.

Keep looking to God in the midst of it all.

On a brighter note—it sure does bring me joy to see you as a parent. It's fun to see you hold your kids, read, tickle, play games, correct, cuddle. You're a good dad.

We tried to be so intentional in raising you. Thinking of what we hoped you would be like or be able to do—then teaching you or modeling those things. I hope you feel equipped for life, like you know how to do the stuff you need to

---

1. Yes, I found this little collection of love notes Amy had saved from our college days. They were not in the closet as she thought but in a box she'd packed carefully and stored in the attic. Yes, I reread those notes. And yes, I've kept them in a new, safe place.

know. I still wish you'd clean out your garage. But for the most part, you seem like you've got a good handle on life!

One day, look through pictures. There are albums and boxes downstairs, plus what's on the computer. Dang, we've had some fun! You were a lot of fun as a kid, and I'm glad you're still fun now! Make lots of good memories with Mandi and Genevieve and Cayde.

I love you!
Mom

Acknowledgments

When it became clear to us that Amy would die, I did something unthinkable. I texted my best friend and said, "I need you to plan Amy's funeral." It never occurred to me that I was asking Kevin to do something he shouldn't have to do. I just knew I needed him, and I knew—without a second thought—that he would do whatever I needed. And he did. He never hesitated, never wavered. He just stepped into the gap and held me up when I couldn't bear my own weight.

Nearly 30 years before, Kev stood next to me as the best man at my wedding. And when the worst happened, when Amy was weak and I was undone, he stood beside me again, a faithful wind who lent me his strength. He came. He sat with Amy, he took notes, and he called funeral homes and crematoriums. He arranged every detail of Amy's memorial service, making sure every moment from beginning to end was exactly what she wanted, in the church building she loved, performed exactly according to her last wishes. (Yes, we sang VBS songs...and did the motions too. And there was chocolate—lots of chocolate.)

After Amy was gone, Kevin texted me every morning, making sure I didn't die along with her. "Get up," he'd say. "Make your bed. Eat something. Hug your grandchildren." Every day, several times a day, he'd tell me to keep living. So I did because Kevin told me I had to.

For this reason and many more, the first person I must acknowledge here is my best friend for life, Kevin Ray Heard. Thank you. You are and have always been the best man.

After the funeral I hid in my basement for a long time. At some point during this time—I don't really recall when—one of Amy's friends sent me a note on Facebook. "I know you didn't save any of your posts from the 'Amy! Makes Me Smile' group," Veronica Preston said. "Would you allow me to collect those into one place for you?"

247

At first I told her no, no thank you. Why would I ever want to read those again? A few days later, I reconsidered. Maybe there'd come a time, someday, when I am stronger, when I'd want to have these memories. Maybe. So I contacted Veronica and said quietly, "Yes, if you're willing, I'd like to have those posts." It took her almost a month, but she was faithful, and one day she sent me a very long Microsoft Word file that recounted every moment of Amy's journey from life to death. That file eventually became this book.

So let it be said clearly, without Veronica Preston, *Hard Way Home* would not exist. Thank you, Veronica.

After a while, I don't remember how long, I tried to read the file Veronica sent me. I got about 40 pages in and had to give up. You know why. So I emailed my friend Michael Warden, a professional editor and accomplished life coach at Ascent Coaching Group. He generously volunteered his time and expertise. Michael started on page 1 and edited all the posts into a clean, coherent manuscript— something I don't think I would have ever been able to do. Thank you, Michael.

After that, I didn't do anything for a while. I just left this book sitting in a file on my computer. And people kept asking, "When are you going to publish Amy's story?" And I kept saying, "I'm not." And in the back of my mind, I could almost hear my girl whispering, "I'm going to pray God changes your heart about that." Finally I decided to lay out a fleece or two before the Lord and see what happened. Next thing I knew, James Taylor had agreed to contribute the foreword and Pete Docter the afterword. Then Karen Pence, Dr. Gary Chapman, and Les and Leslie Parrott had all freely given endorsements. And I thought, *Maybe there's something here after all.* So yes, it's true, without the support of these bighearted celebrities, this book would still be hiding in a file on my computer. Thank you, James, and Pete, and Karen, and Gary, and Les, and Leslie. You people are more generous than you should be. (But I'm not complaining.)

Finally I took a chance and started sending the manuscript to publishers. Many rejected this book. "Everyone has lived through a tragedy," one editor told me. "That doesn't mean it should be a book." I had to agree.

Then Todd Hafer and Harvest House Publishers came along and surprised me. "I will do all I can to make [this book] happen," Todd said. And he was good as his word. Thank you, Todd. I'm grateful to you and the rest of the team at Harvest House for bringing Amy's story to the world.

Finally, I told a group of Amy's friends that this book was going to happen. These were the people who had prayed for us, encouraged us from day one to the end while Amy fought for her life. When they found out about the book, they rallied behind us once again. So to everyone on Amy's Facebook Advance Team—thank you. May your name here remind you always of the difference you made in our girl's life...and her death:

Ali Thompson, Allie Marie Smith, Amber Bray Van Schooneveld, Amy Bishop, Angela Appleton, Angela Marie, Angie Vincent, Ann Marie Rozum, Ann Pugh, Anne Clark, April Jackson, Ashley McMullen Shaw, Audra Jennings, Barbara Ouradnik, Barbie Murphy, Beccy Donaldson Jones, Becky Alexander Helzer, Becky Goodman, Belinda Sanders, Bernadette Gaxiola, Beth Auckly-Cullum, Beth Bailey Hawes, Betty Stenzel, Beverly Morton Kinnibrugh, Brenna Strait, Brook Hickle, Candace McMahan, Carey Wiggins Scott, Carol Whalen Pohja, Carrie Keirns, Caryn Dahlstrand Rivadenelra, Charlene Ruppe Haugen, Cheri Gabriel, Cheryl Wong, Chris Hendershot Knox, Chris Nappa, Christy L. Sylvester, Christy Thompson, Cindy Barnhart, Cindy Cline Whittemore, Cindy Hansen, Cindy Jakel-Smith, Cindy Porter, Cindy Ross Milon, Claire Belyeu Cooley, Colleen Chadwick, Courtney Fassler Walsh, Cris Das Alsum, Crystilyn Exposito, Cynthia L Wolfe Coffing, Dale Gustafson, Dave Goltz, David Bauserman, Dawn Goodenough Canny, Dawn Maggard-Mickelson, Dayle Davidson, DeAnne Lear, Deb Taylor, Debbie Ebel, Debbie L Gilmour, Debbie Mills, Debby Albrecht, Debby Greene, Dee Humphrey, DeeAnn Kaiser Bragaw, Denise Silva, Denny and Philis Boultinghouse, Dian Coldeway Sustek, Diana Williams Anderson, Diane Morrow, Donna Ernest Simcoe, Dwight Magnus, Elisa Hansen, Elizabeth Grimm, Ellen Loser Frandsen, Emily Flick Maska, Epluribus C Cunningham, Eric Wilson, Erma Williams, Esther

Boley, Fred Whaples, Gail McMurray Scheffers, Gary Lindsay, Gary Miller, Ginger McFarland Kolbaba, Gloria S. Lee, Gordon West, Greg Coles, Gwyn Borcherding, Heather Davis, Heather Eades, Heather Meacham, Heidi Fingerlin Lewis, Heidi Fjelstrom Short, Hillary Faith Coffman, HT Goody, Jack Cavanaugh, Jake Rasmussen, Jan Maxwell Kershner, Jan Schlotzhauer, Jane Hulse, Janet Adams Birdsong, Jay Swartzendruber, Jen Allen Castaneda, Jennie Orr, Jennifer Hanes, Jennifer Harris Nystrom, Jennifer Root Wilger, Jeremy Hite, Jeremy Tackett, Jerry Storz, Jessica Brown Van Lehn, Jessica Daugherty, Jill Frahm, Jill Wakefield Wuellner, Jim Nuth, Jim Parker, Jody Wakefield Brolsma, Joe Patterson, Jory Butler, Josh Carroll, Joy M. Williams, Joyce Elam Pierce, Judith Smith, Judy Goltz, Judy Vitkovich Camarena, Julie Flook, Julie Zampino Beam, Karen Harris Lanting, Karen Jesmain Shumate, Karen Jones Kelsheimer, Karen March, Karen Tysoe Muntzenberger, Kari Sanborn, Karol Kinder Ladd, Kate English Warnock, Kate Sabott, Kathi Kaasa Santeford, Kathi-Marc Schnake, Kathy Benson, Kathy Carlton Willis, Kathy Tucker, Kaylea Hutson-Miller, Kaylee Page, Kelli Kirk, Kelly Darby Wood, Kerrie Anderson, Kim Neeper, Kimberly Price, Kristine Zimmerman, Larry Shallenberger, Laura Adkins Mcfarlan, Laura Brady Kocum, Laura Ingegneri, Lauren Kristine Bratten, Laycie McClain, Lianne Bauserman, Linda Crawford, Lindsay Bryant, Lisa Bratten, Lisa Harris, Lisa Leuthauser, Lisa Mehrens Young, Liz Morton Duckworth, Lori Boland, Lori Haynes Niles, Mandi Nappa, Marcella Parmenter-Mancini, Mary Harrison Sims, Mary Hill, Mary Jablonsky, Melanie Joy Russell-Ertle, Melissa Schmid Towers, Melody Parrish White, Michael Warden, Michelle Anthony, Michelle Clavijo-Diaz, Mike Jones, Misty Huss, Nancy Friscia, Nancy Hiett Depperschmidt, Nancy Little, Nancy Wendland Feehrer, Natalie Gillespie, Natasha Pemberton-Todd, Nicole Lyn Vasquez, Nicole Spears, Pam Clifford, Pam Norman Shoup, Patricia Reinheimer, Paul Povolni, Paula Nordby-Smith, Penny Rosen, Randi Nussbaum, Rebbekka Messenger, Rebecca Crowder, Rene Jones, Renee Early, Rick Chromey, Ricky Wakefield, Robin Alm, Robin Depperschmidt-Williams, Robin Parker, Rochelle Maroney Dorsey,

Rod Falanga, Roy Mayeda, Samantha Lucero, Samantha Wranosky, Scott Riley, Selma Johnson, Shannon Carolina, Shannon W Spencer, Sharel Kelsey, Shari England, Shari Kusaba Schwedhelm, Shari Newland Borders, Sheila Ann Spakes, Sheila Kopsell Halasz, Sheila Osebold, Sheila Reynolds Hunt, Shelli Aliff, Shelly Kelly, Sissy Ott, Sophia Winter, Stephanie G'Schwind, Stephanie Seymore-Williams, Sue Corbran, Sue Lerdal Allen, Susan Brinkman, Susan Sellers, Suzi Jensen, Sylvia Nickele Miller, Tamara Park, Tami Lambertson, Tenetia Faircloth, Teresa Anderson, Teri Undreiner, Terri Durnbaugh, Terry Daly, Tiffany n Andrew Ayala, Timia Roehrkasse, Toby Rowe, Tom Tyrrell, Tonia Curtis Harrison, Tony Nappa, Tresa Becker Giroux, Tyson Lambertson, Valerie Hoecker Bakes, Valerie Williamson, Veronica Preston, Vicki Lickteig, Vickie R Thomas, Virginia Friesen, Wendy Fitzgerald, Wendy Jones, Winnie Wakefield, and Yvonne Kern.

My love to you all,
Mike Nappa
2018